ELIZABETH TAKES OFF

Also by Elizabeth Taylor

Nibbles and Me
Elizabeth Taylor by Elizabeth Taylor

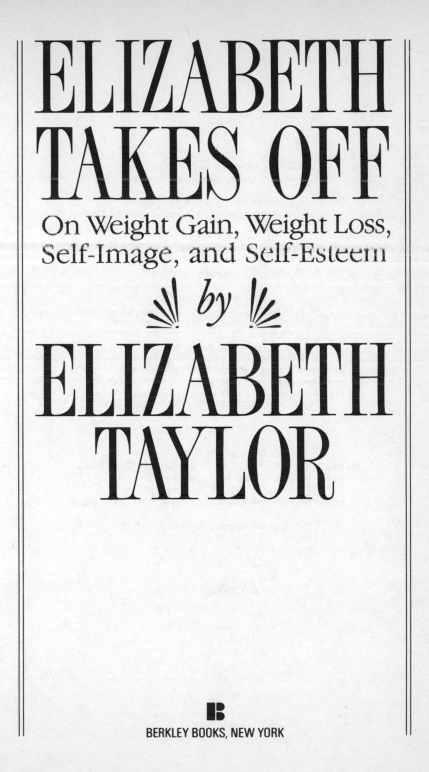

ELIZABETH TAKES OFF

On Weight Gain, Weight Loss,
Self-Image, and Self-Esteem

by

ELIZABETH TAYLOR

BERKLEY BOOKS, NEW YORK

Photos not otherwise credited come from
Elizabeth Taylor's personal collection.

This Berkley book contains the complete
text of the original hardcover edition.

ELIZABETH TAKES OFF

A Berkley Book / published by arrangement with
the author

PRINTING HISTORY
G. P. Putnam's Sons edition / February 1988
Berkley trade paperback edition / December 1988

ISBN: 0-425-11267-5

A BERKLEY BOOK ® TM 757,375
Berkley Books are published by The Berkley Publishing Group,
200 Madison Avenue, New York, New York 10016.
The name "BERKLEY" and the "B" logo
are trademarks belonging to Berkley Publishing Corporation.

PRINTED IN THE UNITED STATES OF AMERICA

10 9 8 7 6 5 4 3 2 1

Flexibook

ACKNOWLEDGMENTS

My thanks go to Jane Scovell for all her hours of help on this book.

I would also like to thank Richard Brooks; Phyllis Grann, my supporting, prodding editor; Sidney Guilaroff; Joy Harris; Sheran Hornby; Robby Lantz; Roddy McDowall; Nolan Miller; Carole Bayer Sager; Chen Sam and her staff; Liz Thorburn; Robert Wagner; and Roger Wall. Most of all, I would like to thank my family.

This is dedicated to You
(You know who you are)

CONTENTS

PROLOGUE
13

INTRODUCTION
23

PART ONE
HOW IT HAPPENED~ A PERSONAL VIEW
33

PART TWO
GEARING UP TO TAKING OFF~ SOME FAVORITE TIPS
109

PART THREE
THE TAYLOR~MADE DIET
147

PART FOUR
EXERCISE
223

PART FIVE
TO SUM UP
239

ELIZABETH TAKES OFF

PROLOGUE

My name is Elizabeth Taylor. For almost fifty years I've been in the public eye, as child, adolescent, young woman, wife, mother and, now, grandmother. You'll notice I've avoided using any adjectives for the stages of my life, and do you blame me? I've been described to death by the studios and press, so there's no need for me to attach any verbal baggage here.

Young or old, heavy or thin, God knows I've never been able to escape my image. Whether I might feel like smiling at my size-six reflection—not bad for a grandmother in her fifties—or want to duck any mirror except my compact, my reflection has relentlessly stared back at me from newspapers, magazines and the screen ever since I was a little girl.

One of the dangers of growing up in Hollywood is that people tend to confuse "image" with "self-image." How you look and what you feel about yourself are often not the same. *Image* refers to our appearance. *Self-image* deals with who we really are. We all know heavy people whose emotional lives are in good order who have an excellent sense of self-worth. And Hollywood is filled with thin beautiful women who are unhappy and unfulfilled, with little sense of self-esteem.

I was lucky. At a very early age I learned to divorce my self-image from my public persona. I had to. I've been before the camera from the age of nine and if I had spent all those years trying to please some great unknown audience, I'd be a basket case. Though my life has been played out in the press for all the world to see, I've lived that life for myself and the people to whom I'm directly responsible. In other words, the people whose lives I directly affect or influence. I've never tried to explain my actions except to those to whom I feel responsible. Sometimes this attitude has shocked the public, but in the end I think they have come to respect me for it.

Feelings of self-worth will naturally be affected in part by outside opinion—by friends, family and other loved ones. Still, in the end, self-image is forged in the core of our own personality. Every woman knows how mood can affect the way she thinks she looks. And every woman who is honest enough will admit that self-image and self-esteem are inextricably intertwined. Please note—I didn't say "image," but "self-image." Looks alone are not the determining factor. This is a lesson my mother was quick to emphasize from the minute I became an actress.

Early in the script of *National Velvet,* the movie that catapulted me to stardom, Velvet wins a horse in a raffle. The previous owner cautions her that the animal was never trained to work. "He is just a beautiful creature." To which Velvet replies, "Isn't it a good job of work just to be beautiful?"

"No," my mother was quick to point out. Not unless you take *beautiful* in the fullest sense of the word, meaning to be content with your life, connected to others and taking pride in your work.

My mother's comment notwithstanding, most women know their appearance affects their self-image, and in our society looking good means looking slim. Weight gain affects our feelings about ourselves as much as it affects our looks. Weight loss can provide an immediate boost to our self-esteem. And every woman knows it takes less effort to diet when she is happy. Though I always adore good food, the call of the double-chocolate fudge in the freezer is a lot softer when I'm busy and content. The Perugina chocolate creams I left out for guests don't whisper in my ear as I try to fall asleep when my life is filled with work and people I care about. In fact, sometimes when I'm really absorbed in making a movie, I'll actually forget to eat lunch, and I'm a lady who believes a good meal is right up there with priceless art.

In my late forties, weight gain became a primary factor in my feelings of self-worth. And when I finally had the courage to do something about those added pounds, I was forced to acknowledge that loss of pride played a large role in the reasons I put on weight in the first place. I can't complain, though. Forty-odd years is a good period of time to be able to take one's looks for granted. And for most of my life that is what I did.

=

What was really starving was my self-esteem.

=

Sure, I knew it was part of my job to put a certain amount of effort into my appearance, but it was nice not to have to worry about the results. Then, a few years ago, my emotional life plummeted, and my physical appearance crashed along with it. It became a vicious cycle. The large amounts of food I ate were a substitute for everything I felt I was lacking in my life. But what was really starving was my self-esteem, and all the food in the world couldn't bolster it. In fact, my expanding waistline just provided another reason to be hard on myself. I would then try to soothe my hurt feelings with another edible treat and drinkable drink. After a while, they became my only consuming interest. The first thing I thought when I got up in the morning was, "What am

I going to eat?" After breakfast I began the countdown to lunch, and when that was over, my timer was set to dinner. In between I sustained myself with continual nibbles, so that in time I gave new meaning to the word *snack*. The dictionary defines the word as "light food eaten between meals." In my lexicon it became an additional feast of banquet proportions.

One point I want to make right now. This book is about *one* of my addictions—overeating. I am not trying to avoid, skip over, or make light of my alcoholism or drug addictions. That is another book—and a big one.

Recently some of my friends have told me how flabbergasted they were by the amount of food I could pack away. The awful part is, I wasn't even aware of some of my gastronomic feats. It makes me wonder if it might motivate fatties to diet if someone filmed every meal and snack they ate in a day. The subject could then watch the movie and see firsthand just how much she was consuming. Actually, I don't think anyone would want to sit through Elizabeth Taylor starring in *Stuffing Myself,* but God knows my weight gain provided the media with a field day. Indeed, during the early sixties, the Burtons' "profane" romance vied with the "sacred" one in Washington, D.C. The same papers that had given priority to the first photographs of Richard Burton and me on a beach over pictures of the Kennedys in the White House now featured my new and unflattering measurements.

Over the years, even when I remained unaffected, I've watched my media coverage with a kind of hideous fascination. I guess my life's been very dramatic, very black or white, although at the moment I'm trying to cultivate the "gray." It's a very attractive color, you know, not dull at all. Still, I can't help believing that no matter what I do, as far as the public's concerned, my life will always be perceived in extremes.

Heaven knows my odyssey from slim to fat to fit again was as well documented as a Supreme Court case. I'm delighted that so many people were rooting for me but I think the interest in my weight and subsequent loss got out of hand. One evening I returned home from an awards ceremony and turned on the TV to catch the late news. The top story was about how well I looked, accompanied by lots of "before" and "after" shots. This was followed by coverage of a summit meeting, a flood and a Wall Street scandal. While it's very flattering to have others so concerned about my appearance that they put me ahead of international affairs, natural disasters and national disgraces, it's also pretty ridiculous.

Unfortunately, at the time I reached my peak weight of 180-odd pounds, my sense of the ridiculous had gone the way of my self-esteem—buried under pounds of unhealthy fat and emotional problems I chose to ignore. And much of what the press wrote was true. There's a difference between pleasingly plump and just plain obese, and I crossed that line.

For the first time in my life I didn't care about my appearance. I was a yo-yo in my weight for the whole world to see, and with everyone watching, I rebelled against the pressure by eating more! My defiance, my guilt, my shame were there for everyone, not just stand-up comedians, to perceive and attack. When I went on my self-destructive bent it was wholehearted, like everything I do. Despite my behavior, I'm not as compulsive a personality as people may think I am; I'm very conscious of what I'm doing. Of course, when you're a public figure and you're destroying yourself, others find it more soothing to assume that you are out of control rather than consciously acting out. The truth is, I knew damn well what I was doing.

I've always tried to be honest and up-front about everything. I've never tried to make excuses or apologies. My motto has always been to be true to myself, whether it pleases others or not. The people out there can't always understand or know the facts of my life. All they read are the results and the results are usually colored by the media. Even at my worst, I feel I was true to myself. At that time I had a certain self-image and in more ways than one I fed it. Now I have

Even at my worst, I feel I was true to myself.

a truer picture of myself, and I am catering to that portrait.

When I went on my gluttonous rampage, I reacted like a great many women who come to a point in life when they no longer take pride in themselves. I was almost fifty when for the first time in my life I lost my sense of self-worth. I lost it because after my husband, John Warner, was elected to the United States Senate I felt I'd become redundant. Like so many Washington wives and so many other women at different times in their lives, I had nothing to do. The image the public had of me, and my own self-image, was shot.

The fact that I made the commitment to turn my life around was a miracle, but I take full credit for the fact that I was able to stick to that goal despite periods of emotional upset and days when nothing I did kept my feet from wearing a path to the kitchen. It wasn't easy. Nothing worthwhile ever is, even something as basic as feeling good about yourself. But I firmly believe that if I could change, you can too. You may say that being Elizabeth Taylor made it easier. In some respects it did. But it made it harder too. For a long time being cosseted and protected kept me from facing the truth about my weight. And unless you are honest with yourself you won't succeed.

One of the reasons I decided to write this book was that I was so disturbed by the hundreds of articles saying that my weight gain—and by implication other women's—was the result of outside forces I couldn't control. This simply isn't true. Everyone is subjected to pressure—schedules that do not allow for three balanced meals a day; the temptation of high-calorie dishes prepared for guests; conditioning that equates food with comfort. But with the right approach our response to these pressures is not out of our control. During the time I took off all those pounds I learned a lot about self-image and self-respect—most of all that I was in charge.

Many people have been amazed by what they've seen me do. And I'm pretty proud of myself. In 1982 I weighed

180 pounds plus, and this morning I tipped the scales at 121. That weight loss is my most obvious accomplishment. You can all see it; but what you can't see is how I was able to effect that loss and, more important, maintain it. This book can't and won't promise you either an improved self-image or a smaller dress size. I will, however, try to show you methods to change the way you look at your life and yourself. Success is up to you. I'm only a guide.

For the moment, let's talk about the most obvious aspect in reshaping yourself—losing weight. Remember, when I say diet, it does not mean starving yourself. Sensible dieting and diligent maintenance are one thing, starvation and abject deprivation are quite another. Being too thin is as dangerous as being too fat. There are far too many women (and some men, too) who believe the old saying "You can never be too thin or too rich." Between you and me, I subscribe wholeheartedly to the latter and not at all to the former.

These days I know the weight that suits me and I've been hovering around that figure for almost three years. I'm human, and there have been times when I've strayed from my patterns of sensible eating. I think all women have emotionally loaded times that encourage them to binge—being bored, being lonely, even simply stress at work. For me in the last few years these times are directly connected to my health. Put me in a hospital, tell me that I must look forward to weeks of tooth, back, neck or leg pain, and the first thing I think of is a hot fudge sundae—you know, the real kind with as much fudge as ice cream. The big difference today is that I'm talking five pounds, not fifty! I've had enough painful times over the past few years to recognize my weakness and, happily, have kept my weight gain under control on every occasion.

They say that not only is it harder for a woman of a certain age to lose weight, but that also she has to make a choice between her fanny and her face. In that respect I'm fortunate, my face looks better thin and I was able to take off weight without appearing gaunt. Unhappily, many of my contemporaries seem to set unhealthily thin weight goals. They think they look terrific when their cheeks are twin hollows. I think they resemble skeletons. I cannot understand why the media encourages women to adopt such destructive self-images. In Hollywood, the excuse is that the camera puts on ten pounds. I'm sure you've heard that old saw. I don't subscribe to it and I certainly wouldn't use it as an excuse to become anorexic. If I go below 120, I put just as much effort into returning to 122 as I do if I hit 125. The idea that I sometimes have to gain is delicious. You see, when I'm working, I can forget to eat. Consequently, my weight

The big difference today is that I'm talking five pounds, not fifty!

drops. At my age, a couple of pounds less as well as more *does* make a difference. Once I dropped below 120 and began to lose my bust! I had to put on some flesh in a hurry! Believe me, it's a pleasure to be in such a fix, but I was a long time getting to this point, as all of you know.

Today I feel a profound commitment not only to my life, but to helping others who might benefit from my experiences. After spending so many years being some movie mogul's idea of an ideal, it's a relief to present myself as I am.

This book is not just to set the record straight as to why I gained weight and how I lost it. I also want to pass on some of the ways I was able to shed my own false attitudes about being fat. Learning to see myself as I really was and do something about it was the first step. Learning to eat healthily and exercise regularly was the second.

I don't claim to be a doctor or a nutritionist, but I have suffered from obesity and I know how painful it is. I know how it encourages self-defeating behavior and its twin, self-pity. If sharing my story will give others the impetus to regain control of their lives and their looks, writing all this down will have served its purpose.

INTRODUCTION

You and only you can take charge of your self-image and weight loss. I want to help by sharing my experiences as well as my diet and my exercise programs. But in the end the responsibility is yours. While I hope the following chapters will encourage you to live in a way that lets you look and feel your best, it is up to you to use these tips and guides to achieve your ideal image.

One of the first steps is to figure out at what weight you are at your best. For women it could be 100 pounds, 120 or even 150! For men the numbers are higher but the same principle holds true.

I'm five feet four and a half in my bare feet and look and feel my best when I weigh between 120 and 122 pounds, no more and, certainly, no less. I think that's my ideal weight but *ideal* is a tricky word when applied to the marker on your scale. I'm a firm believer in going by how you feel, but it's also a good idea to look at a weight chart. A good one takes into account gender, age, height and bone structure, but even the best can vary as much as twenty pounds in one given group and are often accompanied by directions that are confusing to say the least. The statistics are preceded by dictates like "height measured with two-inch heels; weight taken with street clothes." Why do I have to decide which are the right shoes? and do they consider jeans summer or winter apparel? Why isn't the data always applied to the naked body? Then you wouldn't have to worry about the season!

A good guide should adjust the statistics as much as possible to the individual's figure. It should be attuned to the current healthier recommended weights and reflect concern with the actual person and not some unattainable goal.

It is interesting to note that the recommended weights published by Metropolitan Life Insurance have changed quite a bit from the 1959 to the 1983 statistics. According to their figures, I should have weighed 110 to 119 pounds thirty years ago, while today I should be between 114 and 127. In 1967, when I made *Reflections in a Golden Eye,* I weighed 132. At the time I actually thought I looked pretty good. If I still felt I looked good

A *dieter's best friend* is a full-length mirror.

at that weight I'd have stopped dieting the moment I reached that point, but on my way down from hog heaven, 132 came and went, and I truly feel and look better ten pounds lighter.

In addition to charts and your scale, as far as I'm concerned, a dieter's best friend is a full-length mirror. Sure, you can obscure your image. I did. At peak weight, my routine was very simple. First, I positively enveloped myself in clothing, usually caftans that could have sheltered an entire Bedouin tribe. Then I'd streak past the mirror, catching sight of myself out of the corner of my eye. I thought I looked okay, because those fleeting, covered-up glimpses were self-deluding. Don't kid yourself. All the caftans, muumuus and tent dresses in the world can't disguise what's underneath.

If you're serious about dieting, what you should do is what I finally did: strip off all your clothes and stand in front of a mirror, preferably one that gives a view of all sides. You can't lie when the evidence is hanging in front of you. I found that out when I finally got the courage to "strip and survey"; I saw for myself what the public had been seeing for years—a middle-aged woman who looked fat and bloated. Those "violet" eyes were hidden in folds of flesh. It was far from a pretty picture and certainly not a healthy one.

I may be a "movie star," but my reasons for reaching this sorry state were the same as any woman who has, literally, let herself go. Why? I suppose the quickest excuse that comes to mind when a woman's appearance deteriorates is the fact that she's getting older. But not only is blaming your age a false excuse, it is a dangerous one. Face it, there is only one alternative to growing older. It may be harder for women than men to accept the natural aging process, but it is essential for everyone that they do. My friend Sidney Guilaroff, *the* movie hairstylist in Hollywood and my surrogate father since the earliest days at MGM, once told me this story about Marilyn Monroe. Marilyn loved and trusted Sidney and he adored her, but like all her friends, he worried about her. Sidney said that she was terrified of turning forty. "She came to get her hair done one day," he told me, "and while I was combing her out, she leaned forward into the mirror, put her hands to her face, and cried, 'Oh God, Sidney, look at these wrinkles. Oh God, Sidney, am I getting old?' Of course, I assured her that she looked fine but she was so depressed about those wrinkles! Three days later, she was dead, at thirty-six. She would have been sixty-two today, but Marilyn could never have been sixty-two," said Sidney. And here he turned and paid me one of the nicest compliments I've ever received. "Elizabeth, you can be sixty-two, seventy-two, eighty-two, just as easily and beautifully as you are fifty."

Sidney's right about one thing. I am not afraid of aging. My efforts to make myself look good are not attempts to make myself look young. That's impossible. I looked great when I was twenty but I can't look that way at fifty and I refuse to fall into that trap. I've heard that when Gloria Steinem celebrated her fortieth birthday, someone came over and said to her, "You don't look forty," to which Steinem quickly countered, "This is what forty looks like." That's the kind of positive attitude we should all cultivate at every age.

As for other excuses as to why I ballooned up in Washington, I can't even point a finger at my celebrity status. No, even at the time I admitted that the reasons behind my extraordinary weight gain were the all-too-common middle-age afflictions of loneliness and inactivity. Of course, in my case they were aided and abetted by too much booze and too many pills.

At fifty years of age, I had to recreate or reinvent myself, and in my case, because of extra problems, it eventually meant entering the Betty Ford Center. But even before that I had decided I had to get back into shape. Once I left Washington and went back to work as an actress, I was ready to tackle my self-image. And that meant a diet. Even though for most of my life I hadn't had a weight problem, as an actress I had always been around professional dieters. And in the last few years I'd tried out all the fad regimens myself. From grapefruit to Stillman to Scarsdale, you name it and I tried it. I did anything and everything to lose weight. And I did lose weight, lots, but because I really hadn't changed my attitudes toward food, I put it right back on. So my goal was to find a sensible way to lose weight permanently.

Here's something you may not know about me. Once I get into something, I immerse myself completely and wind up devising my own methods. Talk to Mike Westmore, he'll tell you I do my own makeup. Talk to José Eber, he'll tell you I created my own variations on his hairstyle. Talk to Nolan Miller, and he'll tell you that even though I don't design dresses, I know what looks best on me and never hesitate to make suggestions. Talk to Dr. Leroy Perry and he'll tell you I had input in creating my own exercises. Well, that's exactly what I did with dieting. I analyzed the various components of the most successful programs and eventually came up with a diet that really worked. I've gone from a size fourteen to a size six, sometimes four, and I haven't felt as good in years. A word of caution, though, on this business of dress sizes. You might look splendid in a size twelve, so don't start thinking the only answer is to wear an eight. You must set your sights correctly in order to accept a weight or dress size that is best for you, not me or anyone else! I have a particular build, you have yours, and let me tell you, if you have long legs, I envy you.

My goal was to find a sensible way to lose weight permanently.

According to Nolan, the designer for *Dynasty,* I have a classic movie-actress shape. Good shoulders, ample bosom, small waist, narrow hips. Sounds good, although like all of us, there are a few things I wish I could change: my upper arms or those too-short legs or that incipient double chin . . . or . . . See how we all can pick ourselves apart?

In my business, where looks are so important to career, actors and actresses are particularly sensitive about their physical shortcomings, but all of us who want to enjoy a healthy self-image must force ourselves to be realistic about our looks. As we get older, fighting a sagging self-image is one of our greatest challenges.

When I was in my twenties, I just appeared on the set and that was that. I didn't worry about bulges because I was young and slim. Well, that changed when I rounded thirty and headed into my forties. One of the reasons, of course, is that our metabolisms slow as we age. The caloric requirements for older women can drop to 1,800 a day—the equivalent of a crash diet for an active teenager. Certainly we can reduce what we eat as we get old, but neither you nor I can reconstruct the bodies we once had. Youth has a glow of its own, a luminous surface of firm flesh, which time, that thief, alters. And as I said before, all the surgeons and all the diets in the world will not make you look eighteen again, so stop trying.

If you are young, my diet can certainly help you lose unwanted pounds, but my God, you're already ahead of the game because you have youth on your side! The wonderful thing is, once you develop good eating habits you can set a lifetime pattern and avoid having to make drastic changes in your diet as you get older.

We are lucky to be living in an age when medicine and science have taught us so much about the aging process, making it possible to forestall the inroads of time. Our children are much more fortunate than our

In my twenties, I just appeared on the set and that was that.

mothers and grandmothers. They know that eating and exercising sensibly in their teens and twenties helps ensure a sound and healthy body in their seventies.

As a woman grows older, a considerable portion of her lean body mass, or muscle, is replaced by fat, which in her forties tends to accumulate on her hips and thighs and in her fifties at her waist. By the time she reaches sixty, the proportion of body fat can have climbed to forty-two percent. The result is flab. However, this won't be the same problem for today's generation of well-exercised and well-nourished women. Those alterations wrought by age and gravity like sagging breasts and jiggling thighs are no longer inevitable.

Still, no matter what your age, I won't promise that my diet is going to be fun. As a person who loves all facets of life I'd be the first to admit that losing weight is a bore. I'm passionate about most things, including food, and everyone knows that the foods one loves most are usually the most fattening. My weakness is sweets, particularly good chocolate, but every time I pass a mirror these days I know my self-discipline is worth it.

When it comes to actual weight loss, there are no miracles. I ought to know, I spent enough time looking for them at, among other places, those shrines to shrinking, health spas. They are fine if you can afford them, but if you are like me, you'll end up losing the same fifteen pounds each time you go. In my opinion, the key to permanent weight loss lies in the way you eat at home, the habits you develop for eating sensibly day in and day out.

After years of trying this diet and that, I finally worked my own miracles. I heard what I call the "click," that little bell that goes off in your mind and says, "Enough, time to stop."

I first heard the word in 1958 when I appeared as Maggie the Cat in the film version of Tennessee Williams's play *Cat on a Hot Tin Roof.* Brick, my leading man, was portrayed by a relative newcomer to Hollywood, Paul Newman.

Because of the play's homosexual overtones—a sensitive screen issue back in the fifties—the studio had trouble finding the right director. Finally Benny Thau, head of talent at MGM, assigned Richard Brooks, who was under contract and had to take the job whether he wanted to do it or not. Years later, Richard told me the studio was in a rush because, according to Thau, "if Elizabeth doesn't begin shooting by February 1, her contract will be up and we'll have to pay her a million dollars for her next picture. Now she only gets sixty thousand."

In the movie, Paul plays an alcoholic. It was in one of his speeches that I first heard the expression "click." "I got to drink 'til I get it," Brick says. "It's just a mechanical thing, something like a switch clicking off in my head, turnin' the hot light off an' the cool light on, an' all of a sudden there's peace!"

Brick's click is a negative charge. It comes out of the stupor induced by alcohol. It's dangerous and self-deluding but I never forgot the word. For me it has an affirmative meaning. "Click," the sound of things falling into place. "Click," the switch turning on in my head, telling me it's time to change.

The day when I finally forced myself to undress in front of a full-length mirror and see my body as it really was, a click went off in my mind, telling me that it was time to stop deceiving myself about the way I looked. And it was at that point I actually began to work to regain my self-image and self-respect.

Before I really made up my mind to diet I would often analyze the reasons for my unhappiness, balance them against the rewards of a delicious snack, and decide, "Nuts, I'm going to go on for another week, get really fat, and then I'll start." In the meantime, well-meaning friends and family members would ask, "Elizabeth, don't you think you should take off a few pounds?" That would be all I'd need to hear. The perverse side of my nature would take over and I'd head for the ice cream.

But since I finally made up my mind to do something about my weight, I have never wavered from my goal. The difference this time was that I was also willing to face the emotional needs behind my obesity and do something about those problems too. The road wasn't always smooth, but every time I felt myself slipping, I'd stop what I was doing and listen again for that click. Sometimes I'll have to isolate myself for an hour, sometimes for a whole day. Whatever time it takes, I'll force myself to think about all the things I'm doing that are self-destructive. Then, one by one, I'll make up my mind to give them up. Overeating is a superficial satisfaction. Once I contrast such temporary solace to the blessed relief of looking and feeling my best, there is never any question as to how I will behave.

The click worked for me because I was ready for it.

Self-motivation is the only successful impetus. None of us really changes to please anyone except ourselves. Unless you can turn the switch on in your own mind, you won't succeed. But if you are ready, then this book can help. It's more than a specific program for weight loss; it's a chance for you to throw away old self-destructive habits and embrace a more positive way of life.

PART ONE

HOW IT HAPPENED ~ A PERSONAL VIEW

CHAPTER ONE

My personal confrontation with self-image and self-esteem came in Washington, a long way from the Hollywood where I came of age. It was there I first lost confidence in Elizabeth Taylor the person and there I also heard the click that turned my life around. Since I never want to revert to those self-destructive attitudes, it is important for me to remember how they came about.

When I fell in love with John Warner, I was fully aware that he had political ambitions. Right after our marriage Senator William Scott of Virginia announced his retirement and I knew John was determined to run for his seat. The first hurdle was to receive the GOP nomination, but John lost to Richard Obenshain. Though the disappointment was great, I knew John intended to remain active in the political scene.

Then, in August, word came that Richard Obenshain had been killed in a private plane crash. Remembering Mike Todd's death, my heart went out to the Obenshain family, but because of this tragic accident John received the Republican nomination.

Skeptics had a field day. How could a glamorous movie star adapt to the campaign trail, albeit in a supporting role? Theories abounded as to why I dropped out of the entertainment world and into politics. As I recall, the most flattering conjecture suggested I was "washed up" in Hollywood. The real reason had to do with my personal convictions rather than my career. John Warner was my husband, I believed in him (I still do), and I wanted to help him attain his goals. I have an old-fashioned sense of a wife's obligations and always have been the malleable one in marital situations. I adapt myself one hundred percent to my husband's life, willingly and happily. I can be pushed, I can be shoved, and it's okay: I'm resilient as all hell. Though I admit if I'm pushed too far, even by a husband, something snaps inside me and the relationship is over.

Certain aspects of my philosophy have a distinct prefeminist ring, but that's the way I was raised and the way I feel. Outside the workplace, where anything less than equal pay is unacceptable, I believe in the difference between men and women. In fact, I embrace the difference. It's probably because of some of my "quaint" attitudes that I've married so many times. Basically I'm square. My sense of right and wrong makes it very difficult for me to have an affair. I have to be really in love in order to sleep with a man and when I'm really in love I want to be married.

=

I believe in the difference between men and women. In fact, I embrace the difference.

=

For the last five years I've been single and I get the feeling that the public approves, but as I've said, I can't live my life to satisfy the world's need to portray my image in black-and-white terms. If I hadn't learned that lesson before, it was dramatically brought home to me when I nearly died of pneumonia in London back in 1961. At one point my breathing ceased and the hospital posted a bulletin suggesting it was all over. "Liz Dead," screamed one newspaper headline.

During my recovery, I was fascinated to see what the press wrote when they presumed me dead. I got the best notices of my life! People reportedly had pulled over to the side of the road in their cars, weeping! Well, I hadn't died, and the media was far less kind to my attempt to become a full-fledged campaign partner in 1977.

My Hollywood training and discipline certainly were assets in adapting to political life. Still, I have to admit that what politicians endure to achieve their goals makes acting look like a kindergarten exercise. First of all, there's no camera to hide behind, no retakes, no final cuts. You are out there addressing issues and answering questions, not mouthing dialogue. It's one thing to memorize a script, it's another thing entirely to have to organize your own ideas so well that you can draw on them as the occasion demands with both conviction and intelligence. Playing a character on the stage or screen is simply playing. Campaigning for office exposes you to a degree that I, in all my years as a working actress, had not encountered.

When I set off with John I had incredibly naive notions about campaigning. Even after I realized it was a twenty-four-hour-a-day job, I ignored the dangers of constant fatigue and no privacy. Like many before me, I didn't consider the consequences of late and unhealthy meals and tended to snack to "keep up my strength." In fact I began "grapple-snapping" like mad. "Grapple-snap" is a term my older brother, Howard, made up when we were kids, a Protestant version of "noshing." Howard and I used to raid the refrigerator or the cupboard looking for snacks and when we saw them we'd "grapple" for them and "snap" them up. I use the word when I'm referring to extracurricular eating, and I did a lot of it when we were on the road in Virginia. Grapple-snapping became a substitute for sensible eating. During those long hours waiting for lunch or dinner I found myself reaching for anything handy just to keep going.

John was busy every minute preparing for the next appearance, speech or ceremony, an endless succession of necessary and taxing events. As his wife, I was right

═══

Many of my friends were convinced I wouldn't be able to stay the course.

═══

by his side. Like many other political spouses I knew, I was gaining weight and didn't really care. The only thing that counted was winning the election, and since I wasn't working as an actress, I felt there was no reason for me to *look* any particular way or weigh any particular amount.

Still, if I consider my eating patterns during those months, it's a wonder I didn't explode. There's no exaggeration in saying that the road to political office has broken as many individuals as have been "destroyed" by Hollywood. All my energies, all my interests were channeled toward the election. There was no time for or access to the luxuries usually surrounding my life, and I confess I love being surrounded by beautiful things and I love being looked after. In fact, many of my friends were convinced I wouldn't be able to stay the course. "You realize, Elizabeth, you have to touch every corner of the state of Virginia, and some of those corners can only be reached by Greyhound buses." "You know, Elizabeth, you won't be able to bring along a staff." "You understand, Elizabeth, you won't be able to have a hairdresser." Even John was concerned and before we started out he discussed seriously the demands of campaigning, particularly the timetable. Appointments were made way in advance and could not be broken or delayed because even a few minutes lost could bollix up an entire day. Was I really capable of dressing myself, doing my own hair or riding in anything other than a limousine? Most of all, would I really be on time? Well, I showed them. I got up at dawn, rode those buses and did anything that was asked of me. I showed the sturdy pioneer stock that helped my great-grandparents cross this country in a covered wagon and, like them, I kept up my spirits with hearty old-fashioned high-caloric food. Eating, it seemed, even if it was only burgers and fries, was the only luxury left.

Some of the demands placed on me made sense, but some seemed just plain silly. One day a delegation from the Republican Party came to tell me I could no longer wear purple.

"What do you mean?" I asked. "Purple's been my favorite color since I was born. I must have had purple diapers. Will you please tell me why I can't wear it anymore?"

"Well, Mrs. Warner, ah . . . you see, purple denotes passion."

"What the hell is the matter with that?" I answered.

After some hemming and hawing someone else said, "Ah, and don't forget, Mrs. Warner, most people associate purple with royalty."

"Soooo?" I said innocently.

"Ah, well, we don't want to have any inferences drawn from your wearing the purple."

If they hadn't been so serious, I really would have laughed. The Republican Party couldn't make up their minds whether I'd be mistaken for a trollop or for the Queen of England. But, silly as the request was, I stopped wearing purple. I did it because I didn't want to make waves or cause my husband any distress. I put aside my wonderful Halston outfits and ordered sedate little Republican ensembles. No one ever asked me if I felt like changing my image and even I didn't realize I was losing my own sense of self.

There's a sweet finish to this saga. Toward the end of my Washington adventure, after I'd done a lot of serious fund-raising for the GOP, the Republican ladies gave a luncheon in my honor. Just to show that the old E.T. was still alive and kicking, I wore a purple Halston pantsuit and told the audience the story of my wardrobe editing. "Ladies," I concluded, "I'm wearing this outfit today in your honor."

Other things asked of me weren't resolved quite so neatly. While John and I were on the road, I shook as many as two thousand hands in a day and still have a swollen vein on the index finger of my right hand to prove it. The bone was broken and the bleeding caused the vein to swell. In the latter part of the campaign, my finger got so bad I had to wear a hand guard. My middle finger was braced in an upright position, and I had a lot of fun waving that hand around at opportune moments. I kept the guard on most of the time and removed it for the big dinners, praying that I wouldn't have to greet an inordinate number of supporters. Most people were understanding but later I heard an occasional complaint about my keeping my arms behind my back and refusing to shake hands. Even when the skin on the balls of my feet split from so much standing, I kept on going, just adding an extra order of fries and a little more ice cream to keep the smile on my face. If I had been in the army, I'd have received a Purple Heart. With bloodstained shoes I handed out diplomas, awarded prizes for the best livestock, and even stood behind a drop cloth and had pies thrown at my face! And all the time I had to contend with photographers who followed me everywhere, including into public lavatories. In truth, the hardest part of the campaign, a trial not even hot fudge could assuage, was the total lack of privacy.

As the physical strain mounted, I kept on eating. Junk food. When you're on the road before dawn, you grab anything you can and it's usually dripping with grease and slapped in a bun. At the end of the day we'd wind up at some hotel where the food, if not haute cuisine, at least had some nutritional value. However, by that time I was usually too tired to eat sensibly.

The notorious chicken-bone incident was a natural outcome of the unnatural way I had to get my nourishment. John and I were at a buffet dinner in Big Stone Gap, Virginia, mingling with the guests. Then John and I went into the kitchen to compliment the chef. I grabbed a piece of fried chicken from a serving tray and took a huge bite. I bit, a bone got stuck in my throat, and I found myself gasping for breath. I tried to dislodge the bone by jamming bread down my throat. When it became apparent that I was in real trouble, I was rushed to the Lonesome Pine Hospital, where the bone was removed by a surgeon. The headlines were as lurid as might be expected. Naturally, I've been asked if I saw the *Saturday Night Live* television skit that featured a kohl-eyed John Belushi, dressed in drag, doing a takeoff on the accident. Yes, I saw it, and I laughed. He was very funny. How ironic and sad that that gifted young man satirized my excesses and then died of his own.

Chen Sam, my friend and publicist, accompanied John Warner and me during the campaign, acting as a personal secretary. She, too, succumbed to the grapple-snap syndrome. By the end of the electioneering, we each had added a lot of pounds. I won't talk about Chen's shape— this is a book about my weight gain—but there's a picture of the two of us at the Apple Blossom Festival in Shenandoah in which we're both wearing green dresses and we're so round, so firm and so fully packed we look like a pair of Granny Smith apples! (N.B. Chen went on my diet and she's a slip of a thing today.)

The campaign was harder than anything I'd done in my own career, but I must admit there was something exhilarating about the experience. I could be spontaneous in public because I was working for someone other than myself, and the people of Virginia were just wonderful. They welcomed me, made me feel at home, and supported me generously. I still get a warm feeling from them and many times they'll come up and say, "God, we miss you, it was so wonderful when you lived in Virginia." None have said, "Thank God you've lost weight, you were so fat then." Chen has told me that during the campaign she heard people comment after meeting me that I was an okay person, a human being, and very easy to talk to.

In many instances they were much kinder than the media. Once after the election I was given a Trouper of the Year award by the entertainment industry. I flew up to New York for the ceremony. At the dinner, I was introduced as Elizabeth Taylor-Hilton-Wilding-Todd-Fisher-Burton-Burton-Warner. I was stunned. After all, this wasn't a roast, but for some bizarre reason that misguided MC saw fit to roll off a list of my married names. Why do people act that way? Do they assume that because I'm famous I don't have feelings? Never once did the Virginia electorate behave with such gratuitous cruelty.

On November 7, 1978, John Warner was elected to the United States Senate. Our first year of marriage had been spent on the intimate, challenging high of campaigning together for one goal—his winning that Senate seat. I cannot tell you how happy and proud I was of him . . . yes, and of myself. When John was sworn into office by Vice President Walter Mondale, the ceremony marked one of the happiest moments of my life. I had no idea that it also marked the beginning of the end of my marriage.

I suppose, like a lot of people, my idea of life in the capital was based on a lot of movies like *Mr. Smith Goes to Washington*. I guess I expected a kind of federal Never-Never Land where I would help my husband in his appointed tasks and continue to work for the good, not just of Virginia, but of the entire United States. I didn't have a clue as to what actually would happen once John Warner became a working senator.

Being a senator's wife is thoroughly debilitating. I'm full of admiration for the ones who do stick it out—and full of sympathy for those who can't cope. I couldn't, and I don't consider myself a weak sister. After sharing everything with my husband during the campaign, I found myself in a kind of domestic Siberia once he was elected. John turned to his senatorial tasks with passionate devotion and, as was not the case before the election, his intense involvement could not be shared. I had no function anymore, not even as an ornament. Not only is a senator's wife not heard, she's pretty much not seen. A smattering of congressional wives don't even come to Washington, they remain in their home states. Young women busy raising families at least have their children to occupy their days, but my children, Michael and Christopher Wilding, Liza Todd and Maria Burton, were all grown and quite capable of taking care of themselves and their respective families. Such a life is hard even on established marriages, but we were barely past our honeymoon.

I don't think I've ever been so alone in my life as when I was Mrs. Senator, and I don't blame my ex-husband. He never pretended to be anything but a man devoted to public service, and once that service began in earnest, I had to take a backseat to his constituency. After the intense high of campaigning, it nearly destroyed me.

John was up and out early in the morning. He ate breakfast on the run, jamming most of it into a brown paper bag and sticking it in his briefcase. I'd say goodbye, and then go back to sleep. There was no reason for me to get up. I had nowhere to go. Later in the day I'd rise, get dressed, and then maybe read or watch television, or look at the walls, or do nothing.

I had nothing to fall back on, and though I involved myself in as many volunteer activities as possible, I had no daily chores. My chief activities were the monthly meeting of the Senate wives and visits to hospitals, particularly the children's and mental health wards. I loved spending time with the mentally retarded kids. They had no idea who I was and couldn't have cared less. They just loved me because I loved them. After a while I also went around and gave seminars on acting. I'm sure my students must have been appalled at the way I looked, but they were really into acting and appeared to judge me by what I said, not how I appeared. I did maybe forty-five seminars in five years, not an awful lot of activity, not for someone used to a very busy schedule.

If the days were bad, the evenings were even more lonely. John would get home around 7:30 or 8:00 with piles and piles of paperwork. I couldn't plan dinner because I was never quite sure when he'd arrive. This is true of most congressional households. There's a very limited social life in Washington. You go to cocktail parties. The Democrats have their cocktail parties and the Republicans have theirs. Intimate get-togethers are rare. It's similar to the old days in Los Angeles when there was only one industry and nothing was discussed except films and filming. Mike Todd referred to all the Hollywood party talk as "mental incest." The same could be said of the Washington social scene.

John and I never had people in and we hardly ever went out. Most evenings he'd say, "Why don't you go upstairs and watch TV, Pooters"—his nickname for me—"I've got so much to do I just don't know when I'll finish."

This was the rhythm of my life and a more discordant tune couldn't be imagined. I didn't blame John nor did I blame myself. I didn't say, "Oh God, what have I done?"—it wasn't a loss of my self-esteem in that sense. I never took it as a personal rejection on John's part, certainly not on a conscious level. John wasn't doing anything more or less than what any other senator did. I just couldn't bear the intense loneliness, the lack of sharing with the person with whom I most wanted to share.

If I overate unhealthy fried food during the campaign, it was nothing to the way I overate when I had nothing to do at all. If I couldn't have my cake and eat it too, at least I'd eat it, and the fried chicken and mashed potatoes too. Eating became one of the most pleasant activities I could find to fill the lonely hours and I ate and drank with abandon. When I gained weight, I just bought more clothes, and dear Halston kept me in non-purple pantsuits all the way up that ladder of fat. After all, the way I looked didn't matter to me. I was just another senator's wife. I dressed like a politician's spouse, and who cared what body those clothes were encasing? I was just one of the girls. The notion of blending in fascinated me. I'd tried it as a young girl and failed miserably. Now, as a middle-aged woman, I was once again attempting to be one of the crowd. It did not happen. I was not welcomed into the bosom of the political family and my heavy figure attracted increasing media attention. I was a mess and I still didn't know it.

My husband and I were always good friends (we're

I *lost an essential ingredient* of *my self-esteem—my* pride.

even better friends now), but we'd reached a point of no communication in our marriage. Though we lived under the same roof, John went his way and I went mine. He headed for the Senate; I zeroed into self-destruction.

It wasn't only the additional weight; the pounds were just the outward manifestation. Up until this point in my life, my strong sense of worth and equally strong sense of self had carried me through even the roughest times. But in 1979 I no longer knew where I was headed. I was falling apart in every direction. For the first time in my life, I lost an essential ingredient of self-esteem— my *pride*.

For a long time, I closed my eyes and saw what I wanted to see. I fooled myself by looking at my body with what I call "obese" eyes. I truly think that some fat people perceive themselves with the same distorted image as anorexics. No matter how skeletal, the latter see themselves as fat. I admit I could never totally deceive myself. I avoided mirrors, but photographs showed me getting bigger and bigger and somewhere in my brain those images registered. In the back of my mind a little voice would comment, "Oh God, that stomach and, God, those thighs need covering." But it was all on a very superficial level.

When anyone tried to help me, I'd say, "Look, I know what I'm doing. I'm going through a phase. I can't diet until I'm ready, and if you push me, the minute you finish your lecture I will go in and have some hot fudge." I was sticking my tongue out at the world. And because I became the butt of so many jokes, I tried to make jokes about myself before anyone else could. Fat people often laugh a lot so people will think they don't care, but they do. "Laughing on the Outside—Crying on the Inside" was written for fatties. And I wasn't just crying, I was dying. But I never said anything because I didn't want anyone to know.

Unfortunately, many people took my silence as a license to be cruel. Comedians used my appearance for routines and one-liners. They went after me when I was totally vulnerable. As I've said before, there's nothing the public likes more than to tear down what it has built up. I was built up as a movie star and when I became fat the public was alternately thrilled and saddened. If Elizabeth Taylor could look the way I did, anyone could, and that seemed a comfort to a lot of people. I could understand the fascination, I myself was eventually amazed at the way I looked. What I still cannot understand is the deliberate cruelty. The jokes were often vicious and served no purpose other than to incite laughter over my misfortune. One comedian who made merry over my weight said afterward, "Oh, if I thought for one minute Elizabeth Taylor had been upset by what I was saying, I would have stopped. She's got a good sense of humor. I figured she'd think the jokes were funny too." I don't buy that. Those people knew they were hurting me.

Not so long ago I was at a benefit with Joan Rivers, who had been foremost among the entertainers who made my weight the butt of their jokes. When I was ready to leave she grabbed my hand, saying, "Elizabeth, you look wonderful! I just want you to think about *why* I said those things about you when you were heavy."

"Okay, I'll certainly do that," I answered, and tried

to get away. She held onto my hand and repeated, "No, no, I mean it. I want you to really think *why* I did it."

"Okay, Joan, I'll think about it," I answered as I extricated my hand and walked away.

I didn't have to think about it, I knew what she was implying. She was taking credit for my losing weight. But I don't think you can justify cruelty and turn it around into a benediction. Jokes were made about my weight because they got laughs, period!

In the end, I lost weight because I forced myself to face the truth. And even now I'm not sure how I found the courage. The full-length mirrors in our Georgetown home were in the dressing room behind doors that were generally closed. I had planned it that way. I used small hand mirrors to make up my face and I scrupulously avoided looking at my torso. But this one day I got out of the tub, walked into the dressing area, and made myself open the closet doors. I saw myself, my entire self. I saw the shape I was in and I could not believe it. I was obese.

"Oh God, that stomach and, God, those thighs."

It's hard to understand how anyone can let herself get that way without admitting the truth, but despite all the jokes and unflattering pictures I still had taken my "image" for granted. After all, I reasoned, a mirror reflects just my shell, not the real me. I pretended I was still the same inside even though my body shape had changed. But the sight of my naked body and, even more telling, the unhappy look in my eyes told me just how far I had retreated into self-delusion. There in my dressing room mirror I saw Elizabeth Taylor as she really was, and though I always have tried to separate the public image from my private person, I realized that my gross reflection accurately revealed *both*. I could not tear myself away from this awful vision and at the same time I could not help but superimpose on it the young woman I had been; the eager teenager in *National Velvet*, the seductive wife in *Cat on a Hot Tin Roof*, the noble temptress in *Cleopatra*. But the longer I stared the longer I was confronted with the dreadful truth.

I've never thought of myself as beautiful. I've always

regarded my physical assets as a gift—a genetic gift. Now I was face to face with someone I didn't recognize, someone, in fact, I really didn't want to know . . . and that someone was myself. What I learned by looking in that mirror was what all the comedians with all their jokes and all the headlines in all the newspapers could not make me face: I had actually tossed away my self-respect. I had taken my image and scratched it with graffiti. I had literally thrown my gift away. I was no longer the commodity that had paid off so well, I was no longer one of the "most beautiful women in the world," and much worse, I was no longer even Elizabeth Taylor, the person I knew.

How in God's name had I come to this? And, God help me, how was I going to get out of it?

This recognition was the initial click.

I did not want to yield to the grotesque caricature that I had become. I decided to conquer the excesses responsible and in order to do so I knew I had to look back over my whole life and review those episodes that had brought me to this moment. I prayed that by doing this I might be able to save myself.

CHAPTER TWO

I was born on February 27, 1932, and have endured through nearly six decades. Each of those eras was marked by special happenings that identified the times. The thirties were dominated by the Great Depression, the forties by the Second World War, the fifties by the postwar boom, the sixties by a rise in social consciousness, the seventies by the goals of the "Me Generation" and the eighties by what I perceive as a return to personal discipline. Like everyone else's life, mine was touched by the events of those decades, though wherever possible I have tried to choose my own directions.

My parents had settled in Great Britain and returned to the United States only because of the threat of war. Had I been raised in England, my life would have been completely different. Because we settled in Los Angeles, I became a movie star. It was not a normal life course. The demands, particularly on the emotional level, were killing. As a child and a teenager, I was seen by millions of people who felt they knew me after seeing me on the screen and reading about me in the papers and magazines. Some of my colleagues, gifted artists and basically good people, were destroyed by the pressure. They fell for their own press and their lives were shaped by the media's opinions. They never asked, "How do *I* feel about this? What do *I* think? What do *I* want?" They didn't see themselves as anything but studio property. This was not my way. Even as a child, I insisted on determining my own fate.

I'm an observer. I've learned almost as much through observation as I have by actual experience, though it hasn't always been easy. To look without being seen is a luxury for any celebrity. That's why I love visiting places like China or Africa where no one recognizes me. Still, even in the United States, where I myself am frequently the object of scrutiny, I've tried to watch, listen and learn.

As a child, it was simpler. Because I was a "little pitcher," no one noticed my "big ears" or "big eyes." When I first began working at the studio, I saw what happened to many screen beauties whose images of themselves were undistinguished from those projected on the screen. Once their movie personalities were no longer in demand, they simply faded away. Before I reached my teens I resolved to separate my feelings of self-worth from the public image of Elizabeth Taylor, child star. It was a lesson that I never forgot, and one from which everyone can benefit, whether housewife, career woman, mother or any combination of the above. If self-image is based on self and not tied to any role, there is always a sense of anticipation, of moving forward.

I was nine when I made my first movie, *There's One Born Every Minute,* for Universal Pictures. My long-term association with Metro-Goldwyn-Mayer did not begin until my second film, *Lassie Come Home,* and I got the part almost by accident.

My father, an air-raid warden in Los Angeles, was making the rounds one evening with a story editor at MGM, Sam Marx. Marx told my dad that Metro was desperately in need of a young English girl for a picture already in production, *Lassie.* MGM had hired Maria Flynn, the adorable child from *Intermezzo,* but while waiting for her costar, Roddy McDowall, to finish another film, Maria Flynn had shot up and, like so many adolescent girls, dwarfed her male contemporaries. (Roddy said he looked like a runt next to her.) A more petite miss had to be found, and fast. Later, when my father innocently related the story to my mother, she immediately told Sam Marx they had a pretty little daughter who had been in a Universal movie. Mother didn't add that the studio had not renewed my contract. According to Universal's casting director, I had an "old soul" and "sad eyes." In that gentleman's judgment I "just didn't look like a kid." Following up on my mother's lead, Sam Marx put my name forward, and I was tested and hired by MGM.

Roddy vividly remembers our initial meeting: "You were perfect, an exquisite little doll, your features, the coloring, the shape of your face, you were the most perfectly beautiful creature I ever saw and I began laughing because you . . . you were totally unaware."

===

Even as a child, I insisted on determining my own fate.

===

He also remembers that my first day on the set, the cameraman, Len Smith, told me to run back to makeup and have them take off my mascara. I was ten years old. I wasn't wearing any. It was just the first time anyone had noticed I have a double line of eyelashes.

All my life, Roddy McDowall has been bolstering my ego. He believes that being beautiful is a great art form. In his estimation, "Some beautiful people don't know how to carry it and so they shrug away from it. Others wear their beauty with enormous ease." Roddy claims I'm in the latter category and talks about my "composure," a component of beauty he considers absolutely necessary. Once, when we were in our teens, we were on our way to Palm Springs to do a benefit and the bus broke down in the middle of the desert. There were a lot of people with us, says Roddy, including a group of "snazzy" beauties, but as we waited in the sweltering desert heat, Roddy swears, I was the only one who didn't sweat.

———

As you get older, what you are begins to affect your looks.

———

He believes my ability to be quiet, to sit totally still has enhanced my image. But when I was young I just regarded my looks as part of my craft. Offstage discussion of my features makes me uncomfortable. I don't think of myself as "beautiful," I never have. This is partly due to my mother. During my childhood, when people commented on my looks, she would turn to me and say, "Elizabeth, you do have very lovely eyes but the eyes are only a reflection of the soul. Never forget that the only real beauty comes from within." Because she had such a strong sense of character, I never was allowed to concentrate on my appearance. She often quoted the Frenchman who said, "At twenty a woman has the face she was born with; at forty the face she deserves."

I agree. When you're young, sheer physical beauty can carry you along. As you get older, what you are begins to affect your looks. A sweet, tranquil character can erase lines and smooth a sagging chin. A selfish, hard personality can obliterate the most perfect features.

Even when *Lassie* became a big box-office hit my mother was quick to point out that my success, like my looks, was only as enduring as my character. And believe me, maintaining a sense of self in those days at MGM required lots of character. They believed that they had made my career and that my contract held me in servitude, and I mean servitude! My life was not my own. Luckily, my strong sense of self enabled me to deal with tyrannical studio bosses like Louis B. Mayer. Even at twelve I could be as stubborn as he was. Many of my friends could not. While I defied the studio and wouldn't let anyone push me around, Judy Garland never talked back; she followed the studio's orders. They pumped pills into that poor girl to keep her awake, to put her to sleep, and to keep her slim. Judy, an eager, loving and trusting person, never questioned the company's motives.

Growing up in Hollywood never was the glamorous existence you read about in the magazines. Appearance meant everything. I was fortunate because I looked good and was comfortable in front of the camera. But what was happening on the screen had no basis in reality. It was hard work at least six days a week. From the age of nine I began to see myself as two separate people: Elizabeth Taylor the person and Elizabeth Taylor the commodity. I saw the difference between my image and my real self. After all, I was a person before I was in films, and whatever the public thought of me, I knew who I really was. It was as long ago as that when I decided that my responsibility to the public began and ended with what I did before the camera.

On the screen, I ran around the moors looking for Lassie, and raced in the Grand National. In reality, I never could kick up my heels like other kids, there were too many restraints. My life was overscheduled and overdisciplined. When I was shooting a picture I had to be on the set ready to go. And when I wasn't before the camera, I had to go to school on the lot. I'd get up every morning and go horseback riding in Riviera before reporting to the studio. After my workout, Mother would take me to a restaurant called Tipps and I'd have a farm breakfast of two fried eggs, hamburger patties, hashbrown potatoes and a stack of silver-dollar pancakes and maple syrup. And I *never* put on an ounce. Weight was not a problem when I was a child, adolescent or young woman. I still have a big appetite. I think I could happily polish off a huge Tipps breakfast today, though I wouldn't dare try.

Looking back I can see that, between the demands of the studio and my parents' strict discipline, it was an impossible way to grow up. But it did make me tough. I'm still convinced I won my role in *National Velvet* by sheer willpower. I had read Enid Bagnold's book and wanted to play Velvet Brown more than anything else in the world. MGM had the screen rights to the novel and Mother and I went to the producer, Pandro S. Berman, and begged him to consider me for the part. I totally identified with the young heroine who, disguised as a boy, enters the Grand National, but at eleven I was too slight to pull off the male masquerade believably. Except for size, everything else was going for me. Born and raised in England, I spoke with an appropriate accent and was a skilled rider. In my own mind, I was Velvet Brown. But Mr. Berman looked me over and said flat out I was too small. I didn't give up. Just as the movie magazines reported, I embarked on a three-month height-and weight-gain program. Miraculously, I grew almost three inches and gained nearly ten pounds. Of course, it might just have been Mother Nature, but I have always believed I willed myself to grow into the part. Isn't that amazing? But I have always had great determination about anything I set out to do. That single-mindedness, or stubbornness if you will, is as much a part of me as the color of my eyes. The only thing I didn't realize was that in gaining the role I had to sign a contract with MGM. I had no idea then what I was getting into (slavery), but short of selling my soul to the devil, I think I would have done anything to portray Velvet Brown.

"You and your studio can both go to hell!"

When shooting began I soon found myself engaged in another battle of wills. The director, Clarence Brown, felt that when the time came for Velvet to cut her hair to appear as a jockey the only way the scene would have impact was if they really cut my hair. My father refused to let them do it. Following his directive Mother and I insisted I could tie my hair up and wear a wig. Brown said it wouldn't be realistic enough and ordered me to report back with my head cropped. Mother and I left the set still fuming and sought out Sidney Guilaroff, who was in charge of hairstyling. It was from that moment on we became dear friends. Sidney told me not to worry, he'd "take care of everything." He ordered a wig similar to my own hair, and then cut it short like a boy's. He artfully arranged the wig over my own hair and I went back down to the set, where Clarence Brown was waiting. Brown took a look at me, nodded his head, and said, "Now that's the way it should look. See, Elizabeth, you had to cut it in order to make the scene believable." It took a while before Clarence Brown caught on to the deception. But by then he was happy, I was happy, Mother and Father were happy, and Sidney was as pleased as punch because he'd proven that directors sometimes have built-in prejudices that have no bearing on reality.

Looking back at myself as a child, I can recognize my precociousness. There was something inside me that wasn't childlike. In a funny way, the Universal casting director who dropped my option had been right. I was unusually mature. Given my life, how could I not have been? I grew up surrounded by adults and had adult responsibilities. My mother was there, but I had to stand up and fight for myself, more and more as the years passed. I remember one major scene with L. B. Mayer when I was barely in my teens. Mother and I went into his office to discuss a picture deal. L.B. wasn't big on discussion, his forte was ordering. He had a terrible temper and indulged in tantrums to terrorize his employees. Even some of the most famous movie stars in the world were afraid to stand up to him. Most buckled and the rest either were fired or left. Walking out in those days was extremely risky. If you broke your contract with one studio, you couldn't work for any other.

The day Mother and I were in Mayer's inner sanctum I resolved not to be bullied like the rest. When L.B. started swearing, I jumped up and said, "Don't you dare speak to my mother like that. You and your studio can both go to hell!" I'm sure it was the first time I'd ever sworn. L.B. was practically foaming at the mouth. I ran out of the room and into Benny Thau's office. I told Benny the story and he said I'd have to go back and apologize. I told him I'd never go into Mayer's office again. "I don't care if he fires me. I don't care if I never work again," I shouted. And I meant it. Mayer sent for Thau and told him to order me to say I was sorry. I refused, insisting Mayer should apologize to my mother. I would not yield. I never did apologize, and though I continued to work in his studio for many years, I never set foot in his office again.

Even as a kid I never sacrificed my personal integrity to my career. Yes, I had really wanted to play Velvet Brown, but I was never consumed by professional ambition. Perhaps that made it easier for me to stand up for what I believed. I'm convinced the inner strength that rescued me from my destructive slide many years later was forged during those early studio years when I determined always to maintain control over my personal life regardless of studio demons.

Although I frequently badgered my mother to let me play older roles, she managed to keep me in children's parts until I was fifteen. *A Date with Judy* was the first time I put on makeup for the screen, dressed like a young woman, and had a leading man who wasn't four-legged. Robert Stack played my "love" interest and gave me my first "adult" screen kiss. I had been politely pecked on the lips by Jimmy Lydon in *Cynthia,* but that buss was more like a handshake.

Bob Stack is about ten years my senior and I think he must have been amused because I had such a crush on him. Even if he was occasionally patronizing, I knew that with lipstick and eye makeup I looked a good eighteen. My evolution from child star to adult star happened overnight. One minute I was kissing a horse and the next I was kissing Bob Stack. And I loved it.

I always wanted to be a woman. As a child I had been dying to get my period because it meant I was growing up. I loved every second of puberty. I had a small waist which I'd squeeze even smaller, knowing that it accentuated my bust and hips. I flaunted an hourglass figure at a stage when most girls were still developing. Years later, Sidney Guilaroff told me that on one occasion when I walked into the MGM commissary a producer turned to him and commented, "I think I could go to jail for that!" Sidney was furious. "My God, she's just a child!" he snapped.

I never sacrificed my personal integrity to my career.

Sidney wasn't the only one to worry about the way men were beginning to look at me. The studio and my parents formed a conspiracy to protect my innocence. I couldn't go to the ladies' room on the lot without my mother or the teacher accompanying me. They were convinced I'd be attacked. They meant well but it was such an invasion of my sense of self, I felt as if I were living under a microscope. As soon as I was old enough I insisted on time alone and as an adult I have been fanatically protective of my privacy.

Although I had been eager to grow up, I didn't perceive myself as no longer being a child until I was sixteen. The turning point was a shooting session with Philippe Halsman. He was the first person to make me look at myself as a woman. On a purely technical level, he pointed out that the two sides of my face photographed differently. One side looked younger; the other more mature. He thought the younger side was a better angle, I was all for the one that made me look older. In posing for Halsman, I became intensely aware of my body. Whatever the discussions over my face, he had no interest in making my figure appear childish. "You have bosoms," he would shout, "so stick them out!" This was very different from the studio cameramen who still considered me their baby. Halsman saw I had a woman's body and insisted I exploit it for the camera. In one day I learned how to look sultry and pose provocatively. In short, I developed sex appeal, even though I knew that, somewhere inside, the child had still not completely grown up. The most important result of the shoot, though, was that it gave me increased confidence in my camera image, which in turn bolstered my resolve to keep the studio from altering my looks.

From the beginning they had attempted to play with my image. They had wanted to lighten my hair for *National Velvet,* saying it photographed too black. When that was vetoed, they wanted to pluck my eyebrows. I think they lay awake at night figuring out ways to "improve" my looks. When I began using lipstick they decided to give me the Joan Crawford mouth. Each time my parents had stepped in and said, "This is the way she was born and it's good enough for us. We won't let you change her." Halsman made it easier for me to refuse their suggestions myself. I remember fighting a front-office decision to remove the mole from my right cheek. I won and it's still there.

One thing was lucky. Thanks to the success of *National Velvet,* by the time I reached my teens I was a major star. That made it harder for anyone to pressure me. A friend asked me recently if I had ever been propositioned for the casting couch. Never. By the time I was old enough, no one dared.

After my session with Halsman I was much more determined to control my screen image. I wanted to look older so I insisted on cutting my hair. In 1949 I went from portraying Amy in *Little Women,* another child-woman, to playing a full-fledged romantic lead in *The Conspirator,* which was shot in England. At barely seventeen, I grew up for all America to see. I was cast opposite one of MGM's biggest stars, Robert Taylor, who was thirty-eight years old, more than twice my age. Even today Hollywood thinks nothing of pairing older men with young girls, but you never see the reverse. And no one ever suggested that Barbara Stanwyck, Taylor's wife, play opposite Roddy McDowall or any of my other contemporaries.

Filming *The Conspirator* was a peculiar experience. In between playing passionate love scenes with a man old enough to be my father, I had to fit in three hours of lessons before three in the afternoon, otherwise production would be closed down for the day. The entire film was wired to my ABCs. I nearly went crazy. Some afternoons my teacher would walk out on the set, grab me out of Robert Taylor's arms, and say, "Sorry, Elizabeth hasn't finished her schoolwork." And then she'd lug me off to the little schoolroom created especially for me and we'd start on social studies or geometry. Talk about humiliating. Robert Taylor, a wonderful man, was incredibly patient. While I was being schooled, he would go back to his trailer and type letters to his wife. Every time I was tempted to throw an unprofessional tantrum, he would hold up his wife as an example of the consummate professional.

Still, the routine was pretty ridiculous. Running between the classroom and the soundstage, I barely had time to breathe and often would be fixing my lipstick as the lighting was set. One day Bob chided me, saying that Barbara always appeared on the set with her makeup complete. "Well," I answered, "I'm sure *she* doesn't have a teacher who won't let her repair her lipstick in class." The whole thing was bizarre, yet I learned a lot during the making of that film, not the least from Bob's descriptions of a woman whom I never met until several years ago. She, however, remembered seeing me once at MGM. She told a friend of mine, Nolan Miller, that she had walked into makeup one morning and seen me sitting waiting to be done, my hair in curlers. She walked over and said, "That's unbelievable. No woman has a right to be that beautiful at five A.M. with her hair up."

I don't remember the incident. I'm sure I was too awed by Barbara Stanwyck's presence to have heard the compliment. But I was thrilled to hear about it years later when Nolan Miller told me the story.

The Conspirator was not a notable success. The reviews were lukewarm at best, although the two Taylors were mercifully spared as the critics zeroed in on the script. But for me it was an important movie. It marked my transition to adult roles.

From that point on I felt I had three personae. My real self, my glamorized self and the supposed all-powerful self I now began to play on screen. In films, it seemed I could handle anything. I knew all the tricks. But this was confusing. The tricks could not be applied in real life. My teenage vision of the world was further distorted by the fact that I never had many girlfriends my own age. I was treated like a freak by my contemporaries and it made me a little paranoid. I interpreted any interested approach as mere curiosity. When I was young there were kids I was dying to know, but for the most part they didn't want to know me. I did have one very good friend who lived across the street. She was taller than I and gave me her hand-me-downs. I cherished them and enjoyed wearing them more than anything my parents could buy or the studio could supply. Those clothes made me feel like "one of the girls."

If my celebrity status didn't keep friends away, then my protected upbringing did. My parents wouldn't let me enjoy any of the normal activities I played on screen, like staying over at a pajama party, or spontaneously going out just to drive around. The result was that I never relied much on relationships outside of my family. Today there are several women my own age with whom I have been friendly for twenty or thirty years, but as a child I was more comfortable with adults. Sometimes when I was out riding, I would pretend to be part of a fantasy high school or campus scene, but a few hours later I would be back on the set creating the public Elizabeth Taylor.

As I learned how to perfect my screen image, I determined to find an area where I could comfortably move into independent adulthood. Without the usual crowd of peers most teens use to define themselves, I knew I would have to grow up even faster. I didn't have to be a genius to realize that I would have to find a place away from both my parents' house and the studio. After several failed attempts I realized the only way I could escape was through marriage. That seemed the only way I could experience life

In films, it seemed I could handle anything.

for myself and, perhaps most important of all, discover my own sexuality. Aside from the fact I was constantly protected, my upbringing made it impossible in those days to contemplate an affair. Besides, I was then and am now an incurable romantic. I am sorry I did not fully understand the reasons driving me into early matrimony. At the time I just knew I ached to become a real woman, a wife.

CHAPTER THREE

When MGM loaned me to Paramount to appear in George Stevens's production of *A Place in the Sun,* based on Theodore Dreiser's novel *An American Tragedy,* I met Montgomery Clift who had come from Broadway to Hollywood a few years earlier and was cast opposite me. As far as I'm concerned, he introduced a new dimension into screen acting. Marlon Brando and Jimmy Dean are often credited with bringing the Method technique to the movies, but Monty was actually the first. During that film we developed a loving and lasting friendship. Though we were linked romantically by the media, I sensed from the beginning that Monty was torn between what he thought he should be and what he actually was. All in all, I think *A Place in the Sun* was the best movie I did as a young adult.

I also enjoyed making *Father of the Bride* with Spencer Tracy playing my father. Ironically, I had just finished making this movie when I became a real bride on May 6, 1950. On paper, it looked perfect. The handsome son of a wealthy hotelier weds the princess of Metro-Goldwyn-Mayer. It was a disaster, a nightmare that ended in divorce in January of 1951.

I pride myself on my intuitive nature about people. I usually can tell right off the bat whether someone is on the level or not, but in this situation I reacted like a typical teenager. I wanted to be grown-up and on my own so badly I didn't listen to my instincts, though it is also probable that I was too inexperienced to know the right man from the wrong. After all, up until this point, all my choices regarding the opposite sex had been made by screenwriters.

I had dated a number of young men prior to my marriage, from well-known college football heroes to unknown businessmen, but all the relationships had been closely chaperoned. I liked playing the role of a young woman in love, and when I met Nicky Hilton I was ripe to get married. Dazzled by his charm and apparent sophistication, driven by feelings that could not be indulged outside of marriage, desperate to live a life independent of my parents and the studio, I closed my eyes to any problems and walked radiantly down the aisle.

=

I was too inexperienced to know the right man from the wrong.

=

Before our honeymoon was over, my eyes were opened. We sailed to the south of France on the *Queen Mary,* and our marriage headed for the rocks. By the end of the voyage it was clear that my husband was having great difficulty in reconciling himself to me, as well as my celebrity. He became sullen, angry and abusive, physically and mentally. But this is too personal to go into here. He began drinking. He taunted me in public. Then he shunned me. I was bewildered and totally unequipped to handle this volatile situation. We visited the glamour capitals of Europe and were treated like royalty, but the smiles were frozen on my face. I

This is me at three years old,
already hamming it up!!!

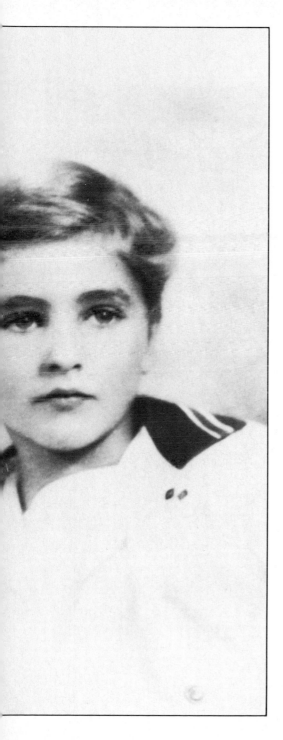

Me at nineteen months with Mother, Sara Taylor, and my brother, Howard. *(Photograph by Marcus Adams)*

Secure in my father Francis Taylor's arms.

ABOVE
Barely toddling, I'm ready to pose.

OPPOSITE PAGE
Roddy McDowall always captured
me at my most natural.
(Photograph by Roddy McDowall)

ABOVE

A cardboard facsimile of me turned
up at my fifty-fifth birthday party,
given by Carole and Burt Bacharach,
and is now in Michael Jackson's
driveway.
(© 1987 Michael Jacobs/MJP)

LEFT

Roddy McDowall and I on horseback in *The White Cliffs of Dover*.
*(© 1944 Loew's Inc. Ren. 1977
Metro-Goldwyn-Mayer Inc.)*

Larry Parks and I in *Love Is Better Than Ever;* learn-
ing to shoot with my brother, Howard, on holiday in
Wisconsin; doing a composition in English literature
for homework after having written my first book; my
mother and I on my graduation day in California.
*(Top left: © 1951 Loew's Incorporated. Ren. 1979
Metro-Goldwyn-Mayer Inc.; bottom left and right:
Courtesy of Turner Entertainment Co.)*

Rhapsody, with Vittorio Gassman and Barbara Bates.
*(© 1954 Loew's Incorporated. Ren. 1981
Metro-Goldwyn-Mayer Film Co.)*

ABOVE AND LEFT

The "eyes" have it! Christopher,
Liza, and Michael; Maria and her
daddy out for a stroll.
*(Above: photograph by Roddy
McDowall; left: Ron Galella/
Ron Galella, Ltd.)*

OPPOSITE PAGE

Roddy McDowall experiments
with his camera.
(Photograph by Roddy McDowall)

OVERLEAF

During the filming of
The Sandpiper.
*(© 1965 Metro-Goldwyn-Mayer Inc.
and Venice Productions Inc.)*

"Richard had so much passion for life through words."
Richard and I at the Publicists Guild Awards, Plaza Hotel.
(Ron Galella/Ron Galella, Ltd.)

Richard and I rehearsing for our Broadway play *Private Lives*.
(© 1985 Martha Swope)

A photo session with Richard Avedon.
(Photograph by Roddy McDowall)

was devastated by my husband's complete withdrawal. I tried everything to keep our relationship going, but he was unyielding. Over and over again, I was rebuffed by the man with whom I had expected to spend the rest of my life. The honeymoon and the relationship were

===

Work and the strong inner core I had developed as a child helped keep my optimism, my romanticism, alive.

===

both over by the time we returned. I couldn't bear to reveal that my marriage was a failure and I kept quiet for months. Around Christmas, I could stand it no longer and moved out of our house. We were divorced in little more than half a year from our wedding.

The collapse of my marriage was a dreadful blow to my self-esteem. And like everything in my life, the entire fiasco was played out before the public. My pride shattered, I developed ulcers, was hospitalized with colitis, and retreated into myself to lick my wounds.

It took a long time for me to get over my depression and, as became a pattern in my life, I turned to work to restore my sense of accomplishment. Work and the strong inner core I had developed as a child helped keep my optimism, my romanticism, alive.

I reported back to the studio and found comfort in keeping busy. If I could not be the perfect wife in reality, I could continue to create illusions on the screen. *Father's Little Dividend* followed *Father of the Bride* and in the sequel my celluloid counterpart became a mother. I was doing exactly what I wanted to, only it was in 35 millimeter rather than life.

The first man I saw seriously after I recovered from

the pain and shock of my divorce was Michael Wilding. Thanks to my ailing intestines, I was still on a diet of Gerber's baby food. Deciding my symptoms were probably psychosomatic, I went out with Michael and dined, danced, and drank champagne to my heart's content. My body healed because my mind got healthier, and though I'm sure the American Medical Association might not accept the Elizabeth Taylor method for curing ulcers, it worked for me.

Michael Wilding and I were married in February of 1952. I was twenty years younger than my husband so in a way my personal life was again falling in line with my image on screen, where I'd so often been cast opposite an older man.

Our marriage began with great mutual affection and enormous high hopes. Even the way we found the house we were to live in over the next four years reinforced our optimistic view of the future. George MacLean, an old friend and gifted architect, knew that I adored the imaginative homes he had designed around Los Angeles. One of his ex-wives told my mother that he was actually building a house with me in mind. He was dying to show it to us but was too shy to call. When Mother told me the story, Michael and I decided to see for ourselves.

The house was in Beverly Hills, right down the road from David Selznick's place. When we got out of the car on Tower Road, we found it was completely surrounded by a big wall and the gate was locked. Many homes in Beverly Hills and Bel Air are protected in this manner. The gates are electronically controlled from within the house and usually there's either a closed-circuit television or an intercom so visitors can be screened. Despite this, tourists sometimes wait until an expected visitor is admitted and slip in while the gate is still open. I've even woken up to discover a whole tour bus in my drive and to hear the driver boldly shouting: "Up there is Liz's bedroom and over there behind the wall is the gravestone of her pet dog."

That Sunday with Michael Wilding I behaved like the most aggressive of tourists. Michael gave me a leg up and I climbed over the wall. I slipped the lock on the gate and let him in. Can you imagine the headline if we had been caught? But we were so bowled over by the beauty we didn't care. The architecture and landscape were perfectly integrated. Both house and garden seemed enchanted, like a scene from a fairy tale. Trust me. We even found a little picnic. The workmen had left behind a bag of potato chips and half a bottle of wine. We took the food and ate and drank in the garden. An incredible vista of flowering trees was spread before us. I think it was one of the most beautiful moments of my life. I turned to Michael and said, "This is our house. We just have to have it." Dear Michael didn't argue. I think he felt the same. We scraped the money together, bought the place, and lived there for the duration of our marriage.

For a long time the marriage was a very happy one, and best of all, I achieved my dream of becoming a mother. While working on *The Girl Who Had Everything,* I was thrilled to discover I was pregnant, and it killed me to have to keep it a secret. Though I loved being pregnant, I had to work as long as possible. If the studio learned of my condition I'd go on suspension, and I couldn't afford to be unsalaried. Louis B. Mayer, the champion of womankind, the man who punched Erich von Stroheim in the face for referring to a screen heroine as a whore, placed sanctions on his female stars for their natural biological functions. I had to keep mum and I also had to keep my nineteen-inch waist pulled in until the shooting finished.

I was in my fifth month when the film was wrapped up. I immediately announced my pregnancy to the *world,* bought a maternity wardrobe, started standing with my stomach thrust out, and, because I was "eating for two," gained fifty pounds.

In general, everything was okay, but there were a few problems—mainly money. Michael wasn't working, I was on suspension, and we were nearly broke. I needed obstetric care and a friend of mine recommended a young doctor. Although I wanted to deliver by natural childbirth, the doctor informed me I had to have a cesarean. I told him okay but I wanted to be awake and watch. He said, "No, you don't," and then told me it was going to be his first cesarean delivery. I remember being more

═══

And because I was "eating for two," I gained fifty pounds.

═══

concerned about his fee, a mere $250, than his experience.

It may sound odd to hear me talk in terms of being broke, but people don't fully understand the kind of expenses a "movie star" can incur. I made very good money but we spent a lot of it. And the studio could always be relied on to screw you. Going on suspension for maternity leave was only one example. If they didn't want to pay you, they'd give you bad scripts, abysmally poor properties that were never meant to be filmed. In most instances you'd say no and be put on suspension. Unfortunately, once the baby was born our financial situation forced me to agree to several films that never should have gone before the camera.

In less than two months I'd lost the weight I gained and returned to the studio. Part of the reason things went so smoothly was that little Michael was such a wonderful baby and I was so happy being a mother. I spent hours just watching my son. Even while he slept, I'd hang over the crib and marvel at him. I remember wanting very much to breast-feed, but working actresses have pretty inflexible schedules and I had to give up the notion. Two years later I became pregnant for a second time and once again despite a pretty hefty weight gain I quickly returned to my usual size six. My second son,

Christopher, was also an adorable and easy baby. Motherhood gave me very positive feelings about myself and my only regret was that I couldn't spend more time at home.

Unfortunately, two maternity suspensions in a row kept up the pressure to accept mediocre screenplays, so I was delighted in 1955 to be loaned to Warner Bros. to make *Giant*. I was happy to be working with George Stevens again and thrilled to be paired with Rock Hudson. Bless his heart, he was the best! A warm, friendly, loving man who gave a great performance.

Rock and I hit it off right away and acted like a pair of kids. We went on location to Marfa, Texas, in August and September. The heat, humidity and dust were so thoroughly oppressive we had to bolster our spirits any way we could. So we stayed out drinking all night and luckily were young enough and resilient enough to go straight to the set in the morning with fresh complexions and never even bags under our eyes. During our toots, we concocted the best drink I ever tasted—a chocolate martini made with vodka, Hershey's syrup and Kahlua. How we survived I'll never know.

At home things were not going so well. Michael Wilding was a wonderful man and I loved him dearly. Our friendship continued until his death several years ago, but in the fifties the strains on our marriage were too much for it to survive. We were so very different. He was extremely British, and in moving to Hollywood he had lost the star status he had achieved in England. We ended up in a brother/sister kind of relationship, which is not my idea of marriage.

We realized our marriage was over and talked about getting a divorce, though we were in no rush until Mike Todd came on the scene.

At first it never occurred to me that he would be the next man in my life. Kevin McClory, one of Mike Todd's assistants on *Around the World in 80 Days,* invited Michael and me to join Todd for a weekend sail on the *Hyding,* a 117-foot yacht Todd had rented. We accepted with enthusiasm, both pleased to get away from the degenerating situation at home. At least there would be lots of company. When we boarded, Michael went off to the bar and I spent the afternoon talking to Kevin. All the while, I could feel Mike Todd watching me. I had a splitting headache, and since I've never been shy about complaining, I'm sure I carried on a bit. The headache probably came from trying to hide the strain between me and Michael, but whatever the source, I couldn't shake it.

Late in the afternoon, we were all on deck, drinking champagne and watching the sunset. I made some off-the-cuff remark as Mike filled the glasses. I can't recall what I said but I do remember Mike turned to me and observed, "Honey, you're a latent intellectual." Nobody had ever accused me of that before! I didn't know what to answer. So I gulped down the contents of my glass and thrust it forward for a refill. Mike obligingly poured the champagne but said in a kind of exasperated manner, "Drink as much as you want. It's your head."

Aside from those two remarks, Mike Todd said very little to me the whole time we were on the boat. Two weeks later we were invited to a buffet at Mike's house and again, though we sat together for a while, he said very little. I was not in good shape. I knew my second marriage was just about over. I was frightened and miserable and spent most of the evening fighting back tears. We saw Mike Todd several more times and I think Michael was more aware of our attraction than I was. Finally he told me he felt it would be better to get the divorce over with and flew off to Mexico. We parted with great regret. I never knew a finer gentleman than Michael Wilding.

"Honey, you're a latent intellectual."

It was only after he left that Mike Todd called and asked to see me. I thought he wanted to talk about making a picture and agreed to meet him the next day in his office at MGM. He sat me down on a sofa, took a chair opposite me, and proceeded to tell me that he loved me. I never opened my mouth. I was dumbstruck. He told me he was going to marry me. He didn't *ask* me, he *told* me. He was irresistible. I left that office knowing I soon would be Mrs. Michael Todd.

One evening, before word of our involvement got out, Mike was invited to dinner by some friends. He

===

"You look a lot like Elizabeth Taylor, but you're heavier."

===

told them he was bringing a girl, but didn't give my name. We walked in and Mike introduced me to everyone as "Tondelayo Schwartzkopf." I could see the hostess looking at me quizzically. Finally she said, "I have to tell you something, you look a lot like Elizabeth Taylor, but you're heavier." Mike roared with laughter, smacked me on the bottom, and said, "I told you you were getting fat!" Oh Mike, if you had seen me in Washington!

Mike Todd and I were married on February 2, 1957. He was twenty-five years my senior and eternally young. I could hardly keep up with him. He was the most energetic man I've ever known and he made our short eighteen months together one of the most intensely glorious times of my life. We sure packed a lot of living and loving into less than two years. Mike was a bit of a madman and, in his way, so was Richard Burton. (I truly believe I can be content only with a man who's a bit crazy.) Richard, who had met Mike but didn't really know him, told me that if Mike hadn't died he still would have been married to me, which was a big thing for Richard to say. Sidney Guilaroff also thought that Mike Todd was *the* man for me, perhaps even more than Richard. Mike was an entrepreneur, a showman, not an actor, and was totally interested in my career, whereas Richard had an acting career of his own.

What sweet craziness it was to be married to Mike. Being with him was like appearing in an epic film. He translated the impossible life I had been living on the screen to reality. He had a great gift of showmanship and a great heart as well. On the surface, he seemed to

===

Being with Mike was like appearing in an epic film.

===

be rough and tough and gruff, but it was an act. He was gentle and honest, with a deeply ingrained integrity that belied his flamboyant exterior. Mike really tried to bring elegance and style to show business. He wanted to make wonderful movies and he wanted them seen in the best possible setting. He had a fabulous sense of occasion, and movies *were* an occasion. He didn't think you should sit and crunch popcorn over the actors' dialogue. And when *Around the World in 80 Days,* his first and only film, was shown, his theaters didn't sell food in the lobby.

His generosity extended everywhere, to his friends, his family and the public. Every woman should have a Mike Todd in her life. God, I loved him. My self-esteem, my image, everything soared under his exuberant, loving care.

Alas, though my spirit soared my physical ills continued, and not long after we were married I had to have back surgery. I was scheduled to be hospitalized for two months. I must have gotten pregnant the day before I was admitted because I skipped my period during the first month. My pregnancy was confirmed about four weeks after the operation and a dozen doctors said I should have an abortion. I was shown a sketch of my back illustrating how my spine had been whittled away and replaced with little "matchsticks." If the pressure of an embryo was put on that spot, it could cause a permanently curved spine. A back support could be worn but wouldn't allow the embryo any room. I listened politely to everything that was said but I knew from the start there was no way I would not have that baby! I told them everything would be fine.

I had to stay flat on my back most of the time and because of the metal back-brace I carried the baby up around my rib cage. She was in such a crazy position, my heart moved over and I was put on digitalis. I hadn't reached term when the doctors decided to do an emergency cesarean. The digitalis was affecting the baby's heartbeat. If they took me off it, the baby would die, hence they recommended premature delivery. I wanted them to give the baby twenty-four hours clean without any medicine being pumped into her system. They said if I went off the digitalis I'd become comatose. I told them I would only be unconscious. That was not fatal, but the child might die. They did it my way, but even so the baby at first appeared stillborn and was immediately placed in a resuscitator.

My obstetrician left the delivery room to give Mike the sad news that the baby was stillborn. He assured Mike I would be okay. However, the doctor felt it would be suicide for me to have more children and asked permission to do a tubal ligation. Mike said go ahead. After fourteen minutes my daughter Liza took her first independent breath. Half an hour later, they told Mike both mother and child were doing fine. To this day I'm convinced that if I had not gotten off the digitalis, our child wouldn't have had a chance to survive. I wanted that baby so badly I would have gone to any lengths to ensure her survival, and looking at her today at thirty, a mother herself, I have never had a second's regret.

Not long after Liza's birth, I was slated to begin a new movie, a project that really intrigued me, the film version of *Cat on a Hot Tin Roof*. Mike was very enthusiastic about this undertaking and was on the set a good deal of the time. The censors were there too. It's hard to believe how strictly we were supervised in those days when it came to anything involving sex. It wasn't just homosexuality that was concealed; heterosexual behavior was subject to almost as many restrictions. While we were shooting, inspectors came to the set to check everything. One day I was before the cameras for a wardrobe test. When a B.I. (Bust Inspector, if you can believe it), appeared, he took one look at me and called for a stepladder. He climbed up, peered down, and announced that I needed a higher-cut dress, too much breast was exposed. Richard Brooks pointed out in no uncertain terms that the camera was not shooting from atop a ladder. The B.I. was adamant about the cleavage and, since he did have the power to stop the production, Brooks had to yield. Helen Rose, the designer, came over and pinned my bodice together with a little brooch. The minute the censor left, I pulled the pin off and we continued filming.

Thank goodness the B.I. and people like him are gone. Not that I'm crazy about all the nudity in contemporary films. If there was too much censorship in the old days, we may have gone too far now in the other direction. A couple of years ago, after my tremendous weight loss, I was approached by the publisher of a major "girlie" magazine and asked to pose—with my clothes on. Since it was a bona fide offer of one million dollars, I felt I owed the publisher the courtesy of a meeting. He came, sat down, and discussed the layout. The next thing I knew, he was suggesting that I appear topless. One million dollars is a lot of money, but as I told the publisher while showing him the door, some things ain't worth it.

During the filming of *Cat,* Richard Brooks let Mike watch the dailies, and my husband was convinced I was giving an Academy Award performance. We'd been shooting about two weeks when I caught the flu. Mike had to fly to New York, where he was being honored by the Friars Club. It was written into my contract that I be given five days off for that period of time so I could accompany him. On Wednesday I came down with pneumonia. Mike put off leaving and waited till Friday. I still had a temperature of 102 degrees. Mike had to go. Three thousand people were planning to be at the ceremony and he would not disappoint them. I couldn't possibly travel, but I made him realize he had to go without me. It was the first time we would be separated. Mike came upstairs and said good-bye *five* times. I couldn't go. I wanted to—I really wanted to.

In the end, my beloved husband flew off in his private plane, the *Liz,* with his friend and biographer Art Cohn. On March 22, 1958, Mike, Art and the pilot crashed to their deaths.

At other times in my life I've had premonitions of danger or tragedy. Once Michael Wilding and I had boarded a plane for Rome. We were waiting for the runway to clear when I turned ashen and started trembling. I reached out and grabbed Michael. "For God's sake, we've got to get off this plane," I cried. Michael saw the total panic in my face and called the stewardess. She was very solicitous though I'm sure she thought I was crazy. We were permitted to get off and our luggage was retrieved from the hold. Michael and I drove back to our apartment. I was still trembling. I couldn't explain what I was feeling, it was just an overpowering sense of terror. The next morning we read in the newspaper that the plane had crashed. Staring out from the front page was a smiling photograph of the stewardess who had been so kind to me.

Another time I was in Yugoslavia, where Richard Burton was making a film about President Tito. The filming was done at many original battle sites, some of which were way up in the mountains. Every morning the actors would be transported up into the hills by helicopters. One day I accompanied Richard to the helicopter launching pad and watched as he, Ron Berkeley, the makeup man, and another assistant climbed into one of the helicopters. Suddenly something came over me.

"Guys," I pleaded, "get out of there." They just looked at me. "Richard, get out of there, just get out," I repeated firmly. Richard didn't argue with me. He never did when I got like that. The three men climbed down and boarded another helicopter. I returned to the house. About an hour later Richard and Ron returned, visibly shaken. The shooting had stopped for the day because the helicopter they had deplaned crashed into the mountain, killing all on board.

In a slightly different incident I learned of Gary Cooper's death. Coop and I were great friends and I learned he had cancer long before it was revealed to the world at large. One night I dreamed I saw Coop lying in a small white room; his wife, Rocky, was seated in a chair nearby. Like a camera my eye moved around the room. As I watched, a nurse took Rocky's place. Suddenly Coop's body arched in spasms. His head jerked back and the tendons of his neck stood way out, pulling his face down and distorting his handsome features. It was terrifying. In my dream I was seeing death—real death— for the first time in my life. The nurse covered Coop's face with a sheet, and sweat soaked through the material. The clock on the bedside table said 12:25—it was the last thing I saw in the dream. At that moment I woke up and without thinking wrote on the Kleenex box by my bed: "Coop died at 12:25." The next morning when I awoke, I called Coop's doctor, who told me Coop was still alive—though barely. I told the doctor my dream. Later that afternoon, the doctor telephoned to tell me that Gary Cooper had passed away—at exactly 12:25 P.M.

When Mike left, I didn't sleep all night. Something was wrong, something I couldn't explain. Mike had promised to call me at six in the morning when they stopped in Albuquerque to refuel. Six came. Six-thirty, seven, seven-thirty, and I hadn't heard from him. *I knew.* And when the door opened and my secretary, Dick Hanley, and the doctor walked into the room, I screamed, "No, he's *not!*" even before they spoke. I almost lost my mind with grief, but this is not the place for me to dwell on despair, the agony of that awful time. I honestly didn't think I would survive and didn't much care if I did not. I came through because I had to, but I remained totally dependent on Mike's memory for many years after his death. I couldn't let him go. I had his ring, which was salvaged from the wreck, melted down and reshaped for my finger. I wore it every day until someone else who loved me told me to take it off. I have had two great loves in my life. Mike Todd was the first.

I have had two great loves in my life. Mike Todd was the first.

When MGM heard that Mike Todd had been killed, a delegation arrived from the studio to pay a condolence call. They had been in the house only a few minutes before it became apparent that the visit was motivated more by panic than by sympathy. They had a film in production and no idea when one of the stars would be able to work again. They actually had the nerve to ask me when I'd be coming back to the set. I couldn't believe they were talking to me about a *movie*. My husband was dead and all they could think of was their goddamn box office. I guess I shouldn't have been surprised. This was Hollywood, where stars are viewed as commodities, not human beings. Things like needing time to be a wife or a mother or to mourn a loved one have no place in most studio executives' thoughts.

That visit from the MGM brass drove me right over the brink. I screamed and screamed and told those bastards to get out. I think I was out of my mind with grief.

My secretary was so worried he called Richard Brooks, who came right over. Poor Richard, I started shrieking before he could say a word. "Oh, are you here too? Trying to find out when I'll be back to work?" Richard wisely let me vent my anger and then gently advised me to save my energy for the funeral. I had to fly to Chicago and Richard was certain the fans would be brutal. "They may even rip the rings off your finger because they'll figure he gave them to you. And," he continued, "as far as the movie goes, it's only a picture. We'll shoot around you as long as we can and if you don't want to come back we'll get someone else. Don't worry." Later I found out they did shoot material with a double. Richard had her race by the screen in a slip, or shot over the top of her head. He never called and asked if I was coming back. He left me alone even when the production office threatened to cancel. It was the best thing he could have done.

When I came back from the funeral (which turned out to be one of the most shattering episodes of my life), I was so distraught I couldn't think, I couldn't sleep, I couldn't eat. I lost twelve pounds in one week. My family and friends supported me but I was almost beyond help. Sidney Guilaroff actually slept on the couch in my bedroom. He was afraid to leave me alone. This was far worse than the trauma of my first divorce, but once again it was work that restored my sanity.

After a while, Sidney began talking about the movie and how Mike had wanted me to do it, and how proud he was of my performance. Then in a gentle, loving way, Sidney suggested that if I went back and finished the film it would justify Mike's pride in me. Sidney was right. I knew Mike would want me to go on living. Without calling the studio, I got dressed one morning and drove over to MGM. Someone got Richard Brooks and he came over to the car. "I'm going crazy," I said. "I don't know what to do all day. Mike said he thought the picture was going to be pretty good. Is it okay if I come back?" Richard asked when I wanted to start and I answered, "Right now." And I went into wardrobe, had my hair done, put on my makeup, and reported to the set.

When I talk about the heartlessness of Hollywood, I'm talking about the people who are interested only in dollar signs. The working people, the actors and technicians, are the most wonderful group of caring individuals in the world. Richard Brooks and the entire cast and crew of *Cat on a Hot Tin Roof* gentled me back into my part and because of their support I was able to lose myself in my role.

My weight loss was of real concern. I seemed to be shrinking. The white dress I wore in a number of scenes had to be taken in more than once. I was young enough so I didn't look emaciated, but I was getting close when Richard Brooks cooked up a plot to make me eat again. In the movie there's a scene in which Big Daddy is welcomed home from the hospital with a festive dinner. His grandchildren, the "no-neck monsters," as Tennessee Williams called them, were running around screaming while the rest of the cast was assembled around a huge table covered with food: baked Virginia ham, biscuits, corn on the cob and a lot of other food I adored, food I could barely look at. I didn't have much dialogue in this particular scene and, according to the script, was supposed to just stand around. The action started and Richard called out, "Eat, Elizabeth, eat the food on the table!" Following director's orders, I went over to the table, picked up some chicken, and literally forced it down. My throat had tightened and become very dry so it really was hard to swallow. Richard kept shooting the scene over and over, from every conceivable angle, and each time he'd call, "Eat, Elizabeth, eat the food." It took a day to shoot that scene, and by the end of it, my appetite had started to return. I even ate when I wasn't directed to. When we stopped shooting, the whole crew applauded. I realized then that the scene was a setup. Richard Brooks had done it on purpose to get me to eat again and the rest of the cast was in on the plot.

Cat was a big success. I'm proud of my performance and I feel it helped me to recover gradually from

Mike's death instead of drowning in my sorrow. The picture was nominated for six Oscars but didn't get any awards. Typical for Hollywood, I won the Academy Award for Best Actress two years later in a movie I loathed.

It is interesting to note that the first time my weight became the focus of attention it was because I was too thin. After filming ended on *Cat,* I continued to eat with my usual gusto. I certainly didn't worry about my weight, and while I was waiting to start my next picture, I even let a few unneeded pounds creep back. In those days few women worked out on a regular basis so I had no exercise program to keep me in shape. I adored horseback riding and I always enjoyed swimming and walking, but the idea of getting into a leotard and leaping about doesn't appeal to me even today. I'm sure it has something to do with the fact that I have a number of physical problems which make it almost impossible for me to do regular aerobics, but ironically, if I had had a serious workout schedule when I was young, I might have run into less trouble as I got older.

In any case, by the time I was ready to begin filming *Suddenly Last Summer,* based on another Tennessee Williams play, my clothes were uncomfortably snug. When I arrived at the set, Joe Mankiewicz, the director, said, "Elizabeth, you have to lose some weight. And for God's sake, tighten up those muscles. It looks like you've got bags of dead mice under your arms." Maybe Mr. Mankiewicz's image was prompted by the lurid cannibalistic film he was about to make. All I know is that I've been self-conscious about my upper arms ever since. I don't think I paid much attention to his orders about toning my muscles though I did drop some pounds and nothing more was said. We started shooting and once again I lost myself in work.

By this time, I had married Eddie Fisher. As I said, work could sustain me during the days. But the nights brought a special hell. I was so grieved, so vulnerable. I could not bear the loneliness of being without the man I really loved. I could not sleep and as the weeks went by my insomnia grew worse. As a result, I began to take sleeping pills. It was the only way I knew to get up at five and not be a zombie. At seven I might be involved in a major dramatic scene, and aside from needing a decent night's rest, there was the strain of playing major emotional scenes before sunrise. Only a movie actress can understand the strain of being dressed in an evening gown, crying or laughing hysterically, when most people are still sound asleep. In addition, even though your

===

The first time my weight became the focus of attention it was because I was too thin.

===

mind knows you are acting, your body reacts as if you were genuinely emotionally distraught. I know now that all barbiturates are addictive, but at the time I thought they were just a crutch until I could get over Mike's death.

It was during this very vulnerable period that I had begun my relationship with Eddie Fisher. He and Mike had been good friends and it seemed natural we should try to comfort each other for our loss. We sat and drank and talked about Mike for hours. My intense loneliness, combined with the nearness of someone who had been so close to my beloved, made me susceptible. In hindsight, I know I wasn't thinking straight. At the time I thought he needed me and I needed him.

The press made much of Eddie's leaving his wife, Debbie Reynolds, but Eddie and Debbie's marriage was in trouble long before I hit the scene. Still, it was distressing to open the papers day after day and see captions under my photographs referring to me as a homewrecker. As I said, the media likes scandal and I didn't try to explain myself then and I don't intend to try now.

In 1959 I converted to Judaism. It had absolutely nothing to do with my past marriage to Mike or my upcoming marriage to Eddie Fisher, both of whom were Jewish. It was something I had wanted to do for a very long time. I was converted by Rabbi Max Nussbaum and given the Hebrew name Elisheba Rachel. Because of the tense relations between Israel and the Arab world, my pictures were banned in Arab nations. Ironically, four years later, *Cleopatra* came under that ban and wasn't shown in Egypt!

Eddie and I were married on May 12, 1959, and shortly after that we appeared together in one of my least favorite films.

While Mike Todd was still alive, he had a handshake agreement with MGM to release me from making *Butterfield 8*. I detested the screenplay and had no desire to play a New York call girl. After Mike died, the studio reneged and forced me into the film. Even though Eddie had a part in the movie, I hated every minute of it. For starters, I didn't like my character. Gloria Wandrous was a tramp. I found nothing in her that I could respond to. I remember while I was viewing a rough cut, a scene in which I scrawled with a lipstick on a mirror flashed on the screen. I walked up to the screen, took out a lipstick, and wrote a four-letter word on the screen. Despite the fact that I won an Oscar, I hate *Butterfield 8* to this day. And that Oscar! Most people agree I should have won the Best Actress Award for *Cat on a Hot Tin Roof* or even *Suddenly Last Summer*. I really gave good performances in those movies, and they were major films. I just walked through *Butterfield*. It was one of those instances when the Academy has a delayed reaction and awards the Oscar for a later and lesser film. It happened when Joan Fontaine was given the award for *Suspicion* instead of *Rebecca*. And it had happened earlier when Bette Davis won Best Actress for *Dangerous* instead of her brilliant work in *Of Human Bondage*. I had been so very ill, I'm convinced that the Academy wanted to make sure they honored me before anything else happened.

Butterfield was the last movie I did under my long contract with MGM and I left them looking forward to a fresh start with 20th Century–Fox. One of the first scripts I saw there was for *Cleopatra.* Although the studio head contemplated a number of actresses ranging from Audrey Hepburn to Marilyn Monroe, I thought the screenplay was pretty mediocre. Still, I sort of liked the idea of playing the Egyptian queen and half in jest I told the producer, Walter Wanger, I would do it if they paid me a million dollars plus ten percent of the absolute gross. To my surprise the studio said yes, probably because between my face and my many marriages they felt I would be prime box-office bait.

Anyway, the next thing I knew I was on a plane to Rome to costar with a brilliant Shakespearean actor named Richard Burton.

Since I was a little girl, I believed I was a child of destiny, and if that is true Richard Burton was surely my fate. Certainly for a very long time he was my life.

Despite what the press wrote at the beginning of our affair, I never regretted a moment of it. I believe in taking life in both hands and squeezing the most out of it. My fifty-six years have known great happiness and great tragedy, but I have tried not to run from any of it. I've always admitted that I'm ruled by my passions, and I can't pretend I didn't know what I was doing when I became involved with Richard. In fact, I thought about it plenty, and it sure was news.

I had actually met Richard years ago when I was nineteen and pregnant with my first child. Richard was making *The Robe,* and since he and Michael Wilding had known each other in London, we invited him to join us one afternoon by the pool. Richard was trying to be charming, which wasn't hard since he was a great raconteur, but I lay on a float and read a book. It drove Richard crazy. I just wasn't interested. After all, I was a married woman and pregnant to boot.

When I saw him on the set of *Cleopatra,* everything had changed. Not only did I pay attention, I fell in love and I have loved him ever since, practically my whole adult life. Even when we could no longer live together we continued to love each other. To this day, my feelings for him are so strong I cannot speak about him without being overcome with emotion. A few months ago, I turned on the television to find a showing of *Who's Afraid of Virginia Woolf?* In the years since Richard's death, I had avoided watching his movies because it was too painful. That night I decided I couldn't hide forever and started watching. As the movie progressed, I was overcome with such a sense of joy and pride. We did something okay, something we'll always have, and how lucky I was to have been a part of it. I had been foolish shutting out those memories and I was so very glad I made myself watch the film. God, we were good together.

I've always admitted that I'm ruled by my passions.

What can I say about my life with Richard Burton other than that it was full of transcendent joy. He expanded my horizons in so many ways. He taught me poetry and literature and introduced me to a jubilant life-style that actually looked a great deal more hedonistic to the public than it actually was. He was generous and not to a fault, but rather to a glorious degree. I love beautiful things and Richard responded by showering me with glittering tokens of love. The Krupp diamond, the most publicized of his gifts, was only one of many splendors. I adore wearing gems but not because they are mine. You can't possess radiance, you can only admire it. Indeed, I've always felt that I am merely a caretaker for the extraordinary objects I've received. I remember attending a wedding in London at which I was seated next to Princess Margaret. At one point the princess glanced at my ring and said, "Is that the famous diamond?" "Yes," I responded, lifting my hand so she could see it better. She took another look and said, "It's so large! How very vulgar." "Yes," I answered, "ain't it great!" "Would you mind if I tried it on?" continued the princess. "Not at all," I said, and slipped the ring into her hand.

Richard and I lived life to the fullest but we also paid our dues. *Cleopatra* was just the beginning and it was not easy for either of us, knowing we were hurting so many people we cared about. In the end our attraction was so powerful we were unable even to try and stop it. Each of us was still married and I was deeply concerned about Maria, the German baby I had recently adopted. I had wanted another child so badly and since I could not have one myself, I adopted a beautiful little girl who was suffering from a severe hip disorder. (After many operations, her condition was corrected. Today she is tall and lovely and walks without any limp at all.) Though Maria was only an infant, I was terribly troubled that the scandal might in some way affect her. It nearly did when the Vatican newspaper denounced me as an unfit mother and said the child should be taken away from me. Thank God, I was able to keep her.

Later, Maria was legally adopted by Richard. During our first year together, Richard and I were both wracked by guilt over the pain we were causing others. Although my relationship with Eddie had disintegrated, Richard had strong and loving feelings about his family and agonized over leaving his wife. For a while we lived together, and though we were hardly the first to break with tradition, we certainly were among the most visible. Eventually, we each divorced and on March 15, 1964, were married.

After *Cleopatra* Richard and I made *The V.I.P.'s,* a story written for the two of us. When that was finished, we "settled down" and Richard's career took center stage. He made *Becket* and *The Night of the Iguana,* and then we both were offered *The Sandpiper.* This was another not so brilliant script and after its release I found I wasn't being offered any significant roles.

There's an old saying in Hollywood, "You're only as good as your last picture." It doesn't matter if you've been big box-office for years. Your walls can be covered with honors and citations; Oscars can be lined up on your shelf; but if your last film was a bomb you are, in Hollywood parlance, "dead meat."

You would think major stars would be immune to this curse but, I assure you, it can happen to anyone. Forty years ago, after a sensational run of early movies, Katharine Hepburn was labeled box-office poison. She retreated to Broadway and fought her way back to the top in Hollywood by buying the rights to and appearing in *The Philadelphia Story.*

Remembering Kate's approach, I was determined to regain my position as a serious actress. For once I wanted a part that did not capitalize on my face or my glamorous life-style. I also wanted a chance to play against Richard in a serious movie.

After looking about a bit we were lucky enough to come up with *Who's Afraid of Virginia Woolf?* which gave me the chance at thirty-two to portray a fiftyish virago. In the past, anytime I'd been required to age, makeup would just dust a little gray in my hair. In *Giant,* when Rock Hudson and I portrayed grandparents at the end of the movie, our faces were almost devoid of lines. This time I was determined to both look and act my part.

Interestingly, Mike Nichols, the director, thought that if I lost weight I would look older, but I told him the only way for me to look more mature would be to put on pounds. And I was right. Years later, when I took off weight after my years in Washington, friends told me I looked twenty years younger.

So for several weeks I pigged out on everything I loved: fried chicken, mashed potatoes and gravy, sundaes and malteds. After *Sandpiper* some reviewers referred to me as being plump, and I had been pleased when one female critic answered, writing, "Elizabeth Taylor, a man's woman, is stacked like a woman, curves and all. What do they want, an actress built like a fourteen-year-old boy?"

For *Virginia Woolf* I decided there would be no debate about my figure. It would be heavy and matronly. My waist remained twenty-four inches, but I got real thick through the hips and bust. With rubber appliances attached under my eyes and chin by the makeup department, and padding around my waist, I really looked like the character I was playing.

After *Virginia Woolf,* I made *The Taming of the Shrew* and had to go on a crash diet. I thought I looked fine after a few weeks, but you really cannot play games with your figure when you're over thirty. When I look back at stills from pictures I made in the late sixties and early seventies, my curves had become a little too generous. I'd always been busty, but in movies like *Secret Ceremony* and *The Only Game in Town* I was getting tubby. I honestly think it was from all that blissful living I was doing with Richard, who, by the way, didn't put on a bit of weight even though he indulged himself too.

What larks we had, but we tried not to let our fun interfere with our professional lives. Our credo might have been "Eat, drink and be merry, for tomorrow we report to work." Even though there were rough times, I wouldn't give up one minute of my time with Richard Burton. Not a moment of the ecstatic roller-coaster years of our first marriage, nor of the ill-starred attempt at a second go-round. We were like magnets, alternately pulling toward each other and, inexorably, pushing away. Creating a life with him was far more interesting than interpreting somebody else's life on the screen, but then I've always lived my life with too much relish to be a

===

I wouldn't give up one minute of my time with Richard Burton.

===

mere interpreter of dreams. With Richard Burton, I was living my own fabulous passionate fantasy. In time it became too difficult to sustain and we physically parted, but those years will never be forgotten.

Later, in Washington, when I realized that the time had come to do something about my life and my looks, memories of those early days in Rome and Switzerland gave me the strength to re-create a new dream.

CHAPTER FOUR

From the moment I looked at myself in that three-way mirror in Georgetown, I never wavered in my deliberation to lose weight. The road wasn't always straight and I had several lapses along the way, but I never lost faith that I could eventually regain control of my life and my figure. Sometimes I recalled Richard's story about the English actress Edith Evans. Dame Edith was a formidable artist, but not a great beauty. Onstage, though, she could appear dazzling. What was her secret? Before going on, she would say to herself, "I am beautiful. I am beautiful. I am beautiful." And she was.

And from the moment that click went off in Washington, I willed myself to be thin and happy again. And eventually I was.

At first the task seemed hopeless. It was only when I began to think how hard it must have been for my family and friends to have watched my self-destruction that I finally was able to turn off the self-pity and lose weight. Even when my weight seesawed I could no longer deceive myself as I had before. I was now irrevocably aware of what I had become and was totally committed to changing.

The second I resolved to do something about my

condition, I felt better. Not overwhelmingly, and not permanently, but enough to get me moving. Of course just making the decision doesn't automatically make everything okay. That's another way of fooling yourself, but luckily, even though I am not the most disciplined person in the world, when I make up my mind to do something I have a will of iron.

Once inspired, I knew enough about myself to realize I needed a catalyst, to help me get on the right track and stay there. I needed to find the greatest mental and physical test I could think of and tackle it head on. Naturally, I turned to my profession, and for an actor or actress trained in the movies, the greatest test has always been the legitimate stage. The two disciplines, stage and screen, require different methods, and actors from the stage often spend many years studying their craft. I, on the other hand, have no techniques. I never took lessons. I'm laid-back during run-throughs and un-leash real emotion only when the camera is actually rolling. This approach sometimes is hard on those work-

======

I needed to find the greatest mental and physical test I could think of.

======

ing with me. I'll never forget an incident during the filming of *Cat on a Hot Tin Roof*. After we had rehearsed a scene containing extensive dialogue, Paul Newman went to the director and asked, "Is this the way it's going to be when we shoot?" Richard Brooks replied, "I don't think so. I think it'll shape up." So we went before the camera and sure enough I just took off. When Brooks shouted, "Cut," Paul exclaimed, "What's going on?" The director explained, "You have to understand. Elizabeth doesn't rehearse the way you do. She goes through all the business and learns to hit her marks, but she can't give a full performance until she knows it's for real."

Much later, when Richard and I worked together on a film, he had to tone down some of his classical stage techniques that were a bit too florid for the screen. Now, in deciding to try the legitimate stage, I knew the adjustments would have to be mine. The project I selected, Lillian Hellman's *The Little Foxes*, was, in my opinion, a damn good choice. Regina Giddons, a greedy southern woman of steely purpose yet infinite charm, had been portrayed on the stage by Tallulah Bankhead and on the screen by Bette Davis. It was a wonderfully challenging role, a lusty southern lady frustrated by postbellum poverty and decorum. I hoped to bring out her sensuous nature as well as her vitriolic greed and was comfortable with a southern drawl after *Cat* and *Raintree County* and *Suddenly Last Summer*.

The part, of course, required that I lose weight, which had been my incentive in the first place. To expedite the task, I went to a health spa. There I was able to drop some pounds and gain confidence. I made a few trips to the spa and each time my weight went down, yet when I returned home, I became discouraged because I didn't continue losing equally steadily. One day John Warner and I were food shopping. At that time I had lost ten pounds and was complaining that I couldn't seem to take off the next ten. John was silent for a minute, then walked over to the meat counter.

"Pick up that turkey over there, Elizabeth," he said.

"Boy, this is heavy," I said, hoisting it out of the cooler.

"Look at how much it weighs," he told me.

I checked the label. "It's almost eleven pounds."

"Okay, you can put it back," John replied.

"Aren't we going to buy it?"

"No, dear, I'm just making a point. Do you realize you've already lost nearly the same amount of weight as that bird you thought was so heavy?"

John's observation struck home. Ten pounds was a lot of weight. I'd really dropped one "turkey," and I should be proud of myself rather than impatient it was taking a while to reach my next goal. Rather than think I was ten pounds away from the weight I wished to be, I should think of myself as halfway there. All dieters need a boost every so often and John's came at just the right time.

My visits to the spa at Palm Aire also helped give me a positive attitude. For the first time in years I was forced to follow a supervised program of diet and light exercise. I realized it wasn't so difficult to diet when food was well prepared and attractively presented. Of course, few women can afford to visit a spa and spas do not present a permanent solution. The real trick is to introduce their disciplines to your home, and it wasn't until I was able to do so that I finally lost weight on a permanent basis. Nevertheless, Palm Aire did play an important role in preparing for *The Little Foxes*. Over the course of several visits I went from 180-odd pounds to 140 pounds, and that's a lot of turkeys.

One incident in particular stays in my mind. I'd gone to get some sun by the pool during lunch, knowing I would have some privacy since most of the guests were in the dining room. I'd almost fallen asleep when I heard someone chanting in the water "one and two," just as we did in exercise class. I opened my eyes and saw a young woman working out. Obviously, she, like me, had come at this hour in order to be alone. She was no more than twenty-one, and extremely heavy. The poor girl struggled to keep going but I could see she was getting discouraged. The fear and anger written on her face touched a responsive chord. I went over to the side of the pool.

"You mustn't push yourself," I said. "You'll get there. I know exactly how you feel. I found it difficult when I started, too. Don't get angry and don't get frustrated. As a matter of fact, why don't we try these together." I slipped into the pool and started exercising along with her. Later one of the instructors told me the girl had been so depressed she was ready to leave. My encouragement gave her the strength to keep trying. That is one of the advantages of a spa; you are not alone in your struggle. But women at home can find the same support by going to exercise classes and even diet groups. Support from family and friends is also important, but as I know from experience, we can accept it only when we are ready.

Meanwhile, over thirty pounds lighter, I was ready to start rehearsal. I didn't know the play would be just the first step in turning my life around, but having a job to go to every day, having people around me who needed and respected me went a long way to rebuilding the self-respect I'd lost during those lonely, self-indulgent days at home. In addition, as the senator's wife, I felt I had the right to look any way I liked, even before the public. As a professional actress I knew I had a responsibility to maintain my image for those who had paid to see me.

I flung myself into the play. I knew that the stage was not like the movies—there would be no retakes after the curtain went up. Once a play opens there's no chance to edit a performance. Whatever happens that night will be the audience's only impression of the play. Fascinating!

Mike Nichols, my old friend and the director of *Virginia Woolf*, stopped by frequently. He was particularly concerned about my voice, which he feared would not reach the back of the theater. I mean, let's face it, I'm no Judith Anderson. In films my dialogue was always enhanced by a soundtrack, and though my voice has deepened as I've grown older, in moments of great emotion it can become high and reedy. Mike had wanted me to take voice lessons for *Virginia Woolf*. I had insisted I could think my voice down and after two weeks I succeeded.

Now Mike was concerned that the demands of the legitimate theater might be too much for me.

"Baby," he said, "you've never had any training. You won't be able to project!"

"Mike, remember when you asked me to take voice

lessons for your movie and I wouldn't?" I asked. "I lowered the pitch on my own. Well, I can teach myself to project too. If I start taking lessons now, it will put me off my natural swing and throw all my confidence out the window. I've got to try to do it my own way first. If it doesn't work then I will think about taking your advice." Well, the *one* complaint I never received from critics or audiences was that they couldn't hear me. It's like what Ethel Merman said when asked if she ever feared losing her voice onstage. "Let the audience worry, they paid good money to hear me."

After an opening run in Florida, *The Little Foxes* opened in New York on May 7, 1981, to a cheering public and pretty successful reviews. I loved performing for a live audience. I wasn't just interacting with my colleagues, but actually sharing an energy with the people watching. Being in a for-real situation rather than appearing in a scene photographed for later viewing sent the adrenaline coursing through my body. If I was able to stir the audience's emotions, I could feel it. And because of the here-and-now nature of the theater, I never became bored. Each time I walked out onstage, I was overwhelmed with waves of love which nourished me long after the curtain fell.

I'd nibble on this, chew on that, and scarf anything edible.

We played in New York to packed houses for a limited engagement of six months, and then went on to New Orleans, Los Angeles and London. There were many gratifications connected with my stage success, not the least of which was my proving to all the Doubting Thomases I could do it. After I announced my plans to do *Little Foxes,* there were very few friends who didn't think I had lost my mind. The situation paralleled the beginning of John's senatorial campaign, when I was told I wouldn't be able to keep up with the schedule. But I finished the campaign and I made it on Broadway, which just goes to prove how little even some of my closest friends know me!

As successful as *The Little Foxes* was, and as involved

in the production as I became, when I look back at the photographs taken toward the end of the run, it's patently obvious I had been gaining weight. At the outset I managed to discipline myself but by the time *Little Foxes* closed I was heavy again. One of the reasons had to do with my return to grapple-snapping. My dressing room doubled as a dining room. I'd nibble on this, chew on that, and scarf anything edible. It is exhilarating to appear on the stage but it's also enervating. I thought all my onstage activity was burning off all the calories accumulated during intermission. The sweat poured off and with it, I was certain, went the weight. Well, the truth is, all the exerted energy in the world couldn't sizzle off the pounds I was packing on, and alas, there's plenty of incriminating evidence. After eighteen months boredom was setting in.

I recently came across one picture taken at my fiftieth birthday party during the London engagement of the play. It made me shiver. I'm dressed all in white and my eyes have disappeared into suet. I'm still wearing stage makeup and I look for all the world like a drag queen. I did my best to deny the truth, but my self-image suffered badly and I knew the time had come to take action again.

Not surprisingly, my marriage did not survive the run of *Little Foxes*. Even before I decided to do the play, John and I were aware of our problems, and I think it was clear to us both when I went to New York that we would eventually split. The straw that broke the camel's back came the day he told me he'd sold the house and bought an apartment at Watergate. He said I had to get rid of all my animals. Click! That was the coup de grace. I felt I deserved more consideration. It wasn't as though I hadn't contributed to our lives, for Pete's sake. I'd even sold the diamond engagement ring Mike Todd gave me and the Taylor-Burton diamond to keep up with our expenses. And now I wasn't even allowed to keep my pets.

Consequently, when I returned from the London run of the play, I decided to move to Los Angeles. I adore visiting London and New York, but I guess Hollywood really is my home. I love the climate. I love the rural areas so close to town. And today there are no set social rules. Once it was very much a company town. Now it's a big city. Best of all, because there are so many movie stars, it's the place where I have the most personal freedom. Strangers tend to keep their distance and allow me to keep mine. I don't worry so much about the mob scenes that can develop in other cities. Even in New York I've nearly been pulled to pieces. And you wouldn't believe the people who are roughest with me—women my own age or older. One time I went into a department store to pick up a lipstick, and word got around I was in the store. The next thing I knew, I was surrounded. They had to call the police to get me out. In L.A., people are wonderful. They just call out, "Hi, Liz," and leave me alone.

So having made my decision in 1982, I came home. I didn't look or feel quite the way I'd hoped, but I felt a helluva lot better than I had in many years. I had come a long way from Washington and accomplished much of what I set out to do. Despite my weight gain I was determined to keep busy and take control of my future.

Since my track record was good, I went into another theatrical project, a project that reunited me, professionally, with one of the most important persons in my life: Richard Burton. It was a play that began with great hope and ended in great sorrow. But out of that sorrow came self-knowledge and out of that knowledge came triumph.

CHAPTER FIVE

A s soon as I announced I was ready to do another play I was flooded with projects. One that intrigued me was Tennessee Williams's *Sweet Bird of Youth*. I knew the role of the fading southern belle would suit me. Geraldine Page had played it on stage and screen opposite young Paul Newman. There was a catch, however. There was no part for Richard. I would have no problem playing the mature woman, but Richard was too old for Chance, the young drifter. In retrospect, we would have been better off abandoning our plan to co-star, but at the time I refused to consider the idea. Someone suggested we do a revival of *Who's Afraid of Virginia Woolf?* but we'd already done it, and we wanted something new, a play showing two middle-aged people who though miles down the road from their once all-consuming passion still cared deeply for each other. That's when we came up with Noël Coward's *Private Lives*.

The project was doomed from the start. I was not in good shape and neither was Richard. Worse yet, we were both miscast. We should have done a drama, not an English drawing room comedy. The experience was devastating, certainly for me, and I'm sure for Richard. Richard got married during the play's run, adding to the strain. I began to crack. My worst habits surfaced. I began overeating, drinking, and taking pills. I never touched a drop before the show, I was too professional for that, but the minute the curtain went down, Jack Daniel's was waiting in the wings. After the performance

===

My worst habits surfaced. I began overeating, drinking, and taking pills.

===

Richard and I would go out—separately: he with his wife and friends, and I with my gang, usually culled from the cast and crew. Whatever city we were playing—Boston, Philadelphia, Washington—we'd find a late-night restaurant and settle in, sometimes until four in the morning. It became a twenty-four-hour nightmare. It didn't matter that we didn't get good reviews. We still played to packed houses. No one was coming to see the English drawing room comedy anyway. Everyone bought tickets to watch high-camp "Liz and Dick." And we gave them what they wanted. I wanted to stop, to put an end to this torture, but the contract had to be fulfilled.

Private Lives closed on November 6, 1983, and one month later, on December 5, I entered the Betty Ford Center.

Up until this time, I'd thought I had reached my lowest ebb in Washington and was securely set on the road back. When I got the click in Georgetown I had found the strength to restructure my life. And God help me, it wasn't enough. Within a few short years I was, once again, lonely and frightened, only this time I *knew* I could not fool myself anymore. I certainly wasn't as obese as I had been, and I felt a lot better about the way I looked, but I was wracked with self-doubt. And to add to the agony, my physical ailments flared up with a vengeance. My spine acted up, putting me flat on my back, and I was awash in self-pity and self-disgust. I retreated into my home and shut the door. Thank God, this time my family and friends wouldn't let me get away with it.

During one of many hospital stays, a family intervention took place in my room. My children, my brother, a few intimate friends made me face the facts. I was assured of their love while at the same time I was told how my behavior had affected them, and of their real fears that I was killing myself. I listened in total silence. I remember being shocked. I couldn't believe what I had become. At the end, they said reservations had been made for me at the Betty Ford Center and they wanted me to go.

I listened and then asked them to leave me alone for a couple of hours. I knew myself well enough to realize I wouldn't have the determination to follow through unless the decision was *mine*.

Everyone bought tickets to watch high-camp "Liz and Dick."

When they had gone, I went over every word that had been said. And after much deliberation, I thought, okay, it's time. I called them back and said I was ready.

I checked in several days later. Although we tried to keep it quiet, my admission naturally made headlines. As a matter of fact, several days after I arrived, I called Betty and told her I had a feeling the story was about to break. It's hard to explain, but I have a sixth sense when it comes to the media. I felt an unauthorized presence at the clinic and it turned out I was absolutely right.

A reporter had been snooping around, but before he could file his story, we beat him to the punch and the Betty Ford Center made the announcement.

In the end, whatever the media said didn't matter. All that counted was that I was there and getting the help I needed. The Betty Ford Center changed my life. Being there filled me with the desire to live my life to the fullest. It forced me to pull my life together, willingly and happily. I had to face things at Betty Ford I never had to face before. I learned that I had spent years squelching my real feelings for fear they'd become public. All the years of covering up the pain and keeping it quiet had created a lot of scar tissue.

At Betty Ford I was able to strip away all my protective layers and deal with the essential core. It is a very healthy process. You learn to look at what you really are and live with it. You reveal the things that are painful and by releasing them you release yourself. The entire process of tearing down and rebuilding on a solid foundation of self-awareness makes it possible for almost anyone to conquer those demons.

===

All that counted was that I was there and getting the help I needed.

===

I was fortunate to have Betty Ford herself as my sponsor. I simply must say a word about this remarkable woman. When I revealed my drug and alcohol dependency many people said, "Oh well, just another movie actress who's been married too many times." Betty Ford could never be classified that way. She was the First Lady of this country, a woman admired throughout the world. The courage and humility it took for her to reveal the darkest side of her life gave people like me the inspiration to do the same.

All the time I was at the center, everything was upbeat, and when I left I was filled with positive energy to continue losing weight as part of my overall program to regaining self-esteem and self-respect. Mentally I was in top condition. Physically I was still a woman who'd been doing a lot of harm to her body for an awfully long time. Happily, God made me incredibly resilient and I was able to bounce back. In fact, when someone recently

---

Why shouldn't my outward appearance match all the good feelings inside?

---

asked me what was my proudest accomplishment, I said with all sincerity, "Just being alive."

At one point Richard saw a picture of me after I left the center and called to tell me how impressed he was with what I had done. I told him I wished we could have gone together while still married.

While at the center, the staff advised us not to diet, because they don't want you to take on too many things at once, but I actually lost eleven pounds of bloat simply because I stopped drinking. When I got back home, my body craved sugar, but I wouldn't supply it with alcohol. Well, I became a chocoholic and put on fifteen pounds of pure, solid fat! There was sugar to burn. Fortunately, I was able to pull myself out of this mess. I may have been fat but I was mentally and emotionally fit, thanks to my Betty Ford Center stay. I didn't need to drink and I felt so good about that, I began to think, well, why shouldn't my outward appearance match all the good feelings inside? Why not enjoy everything that

God gave me, including my natural physical gifts? By God, I could control my eating, too! And that's just what I did.

Everything seemed to fall into place. For the first time since I'd begun struggling with my weight, I adopted a sensible and consistent attitude toward food.

No more crash diets and no more binges. Finally I learned to eat sensibly and healthily day in and day out, month after month. Sure, I indulge from time to time in fried chicken or hot fudge sundaes, but they are controlled indulgences. I don't go hog-wild and I don't feel guilty. Neither does my weight fluctuate over five pounds.

While I was dropping weight, I was also freeing myself in other ways, ways that might seem silly but were important to me. For example, I decided to become a blonde. In *Private Lives* the script had called for a blond wig. Now I decided to color my own hair. I'll admit that's hardly an earth-shattering decision, but I got a kick out of it precisely because it was just the kind of thing I had never been able to do. When I was young, I couldn't change anything about my appearance without getting permission from the studio. They had once insisted I bleach my hair to play Amy March in *Little Women*. This time I did it myself. Afterward I realized it was probably a mistake. I was meant to be a brunette. Still, just feeling free to experiment with my looks, something I'd been denied all the years I was growing up, helped me realize that for the first time in my life I was responsible to no one except myself. In my teens and twenties, I'd had the responsibilities of a woman. Now, with no long-term studio contract and with my kids grown up, I had to think only about what was best for me. You have no idea how exhilarating it was to be able to call the shots, even on something as dumb as dyeing my hair. Basically, I think that's why I'm enjoying being single. I'm not catering to someone else. If I want to eat at eight, I eat at eight. If I want to eat at six, I eat at six. I'm not adjusting my schedule to fit someone else's rhythms.

Sometimes I think that the fact I was living alone during the months I was following the most rigorous phase of my diet and exercise program made it easier to lose weight. Still, I know that once I made up my mind even a houseful of ravenous kids and a husband demanding three meals a day wouldn't have stopped me.

But I must admit that the wonderful serenity of the new house I bought when I moved back to Los Angeles helped keep my emotions on an even keel and encouraged me to stick to my resolve.

Finding that house was a real stroke of luck. I've always loved Bel Air because of its rural feeling, but the realtor taking me around kept trying to tell me which properties I would like. I tried not to listen since the only way I can tell if a house is right for me is to soak up its ambience. When we reached our second stop I asked the woman to remain outside and went through the house myself. It was perfect. To the realtor's surprise I walked out five minutes later and said, "I'll take it."

I have never regretted the decision. It is comfortable, peaceful and private. The years I have lived here have brought me much joy. From my bedroom window I can look out on the lovely garden where one tree in particular inspires me if I am down. It has an exotic, magical quality like the woods that come alive in *The Wizard of Oz*. Obviously it was worked over in a nursery. Its three roots were twined around each other and then bent over to hug the ground. I think tree surgeons use the term "tortured." Whenever I contemplate this mangled bit of nature, I'm awed by the way it survives and renews itself each spring in a splendid finery of greens and blossoms. Anytime I've wanted to give in to any of the dark forces in my life—from overeating to self-pity—I look at that tree and find the courage to go on.

In general, life in the last few years has been good to me. I work when I want to, spend a good deal of time promoting my favorite charities, and enjoy socializing. Given the public nature of my life, the last activity hasn't always been easy. I don't think any man can help but know about my passionate marriages to Mike Todd and Richard Burton. Those are powerful names for anyone to contend with. I know. They were for me.

And quite aside from the past, going out with a celebrity can be pretty traumatic. A man has to be damned sure of himself to be able to handle the commotion.

Not long ago, I went on a dinner date to an elegant restaurant on Sunset Boulevard. My friend and I finished eating and were about to leave when the maître d' came over to the table and apologetically suggested we leave by the back door.

"Believe me, Miss Taylor, I didn't say anything, but you know how it is, someone saw you come in and now the photographers are crawling all over the sidewalk."

My heart sank. My date, a really nice person, was not in the movie business and was unused to the Hollywood paparazzi. "Why don't we just slip out the back," I suggested. Instead of agreeing, he surprised me by saying, "Look, why should you have to sneak out of here like a criminal? We'll walk out the way we came in." I thought to myself, "Well done, sir."

On another occasion I went for dinner with a man I had known for years but never really "dated." He drove up to the restaurant, parked the car, got out, and started walking toward the door. He was almost inside the restaurant when he realized I was still sitting in the car. The expression on his face was priceless as he looked back at me. I was laughing but I would not leave that car until he came around and opened the door for me.

These were good dating experiences. I've had the other kind too. There are a lot of men who will ask me out just to be seen with a celebrity. They are not really interested in Elizabeth the woman. Fortunately I've become pretty adept at sizing up such losers.

Still, the truth of the matter is, I feel pretty strange to be dating at my age. When I grew up women in their fifties were generally grandmothers who stayed at home with their husbands and were visited by their children and grandchildren. They weren't running about town with a variety of men. Well, I've had to rethink my views and, believe me, I'm not alone. There are millions of middle-aged single women who are leading totally different lives from those of their parents. Many women in this position become insecure because some pretty fundamental props—home, husband, family—aren't there. I understand that feeling, but I can tell you from experience, you won't be able to handle your insecurities until you face them.

I have done just that in almost all areas of my life, and as you can see, it's worked. I've come a long way from the obese woman with sad eyes who finally confronted her damaged self-image and self-esteem eight years ago. One event in particular seems to sum up my new life.

In February 1987, to celebrate my fifty-fifth birthday, Carole Bayer Sager and Burt Bacharach hosted a party for me at their Bel Air home. One hundred fifty people were there and it was one of the most incredible events I've ever attended.

At the entrance to the Bacharachs' house stood a life-size cardboard figure of myself at twelve, holding up a sign announcing "Valet Parking."

===

There are a lot of men who will ask me out just to be seen with a celebrity.

===

Inside the house was a throng of friends, many of whom have known me since I was a little girl and all of whom have stood by me through thick and thin!

I thought about their incredible loyalty as I was getting dressed for the party in the beautiful low-cut white silk dress designed by Nolan Miller. As I ran the zipper past the twenty-two inch waist I wondered how many of those friends could have believed I would fit into that dress just a few short years ago. "Hey," I smiled, looking at my reflection. "That's not bad for a fifty-five-year-old woman."

Fifty-five years! I've sure come a long way since *Lassie,* though the party invitation featured us together the way we had looked back in 1946. As I entered the house I smiled to see some of the people I've known since the day I walked on the Metro-Goldwyn-Mayer lot. MGM as we knew it is gone, but much of the real spirit of

≡

Fifty-five years! I've sure come a long way since Lassie.

≡

Hollywood was represented, from Bette Davis and Sidney Guilaroff to Jennifer Jones and Michael Jackson.

A lot of my old "boyfriends" were there, too, like Arthur Loew, whom I'd dated in the fifties. My escort for the evening was George Hamilton, a very special person in my life. My mother, who had come up from Palm Springs for the occasion, was delighted with everything, from the life-size valet parking sign to the final serenade. She's ninety-one and still looks so beautiful. I really have been blessed.

The theme of the party was diamonds. Even the picture of Lassie on the invitation had been bedecked with them. Diamonds (okay, rhinestones) were festooned around my neck and a giant stone was placed on my ring finger. Every place card had a huge gleaming fake diamond in the center, and diamondlike lights sparkled at the top of the clear tent that covered the courtyard where the tables were set up.

At the end of the party, each woman was given a ring, a cut-glass Cartier reproduction of the Taylor-Burton diamond, inscribed "E. T. 2/27/87." Can you imagine all of us flashing those gigantic "diamonds." "Camp" yes, but I loved it!

My turning fifty-five seems a nice spot to end my story and turn to the diet and exercise portion of this book. I admit that today the "new" Elizabeth Taylor is my greatest role. At fifty-five years old, by golly, I've become a sex symbol again! I hope, however, that my revitalized self-image symbolizes more than that. I believe my comeback is a victory for anyone who has ever felt unloved, unwanted and ineffectual.

Today I revel in my newfound independence. My image radiates a new self-confidence. My physical recovery, like my mental recovery, stems from a sense of strength, not any frantic need for self-improvement.

Slowly but surely I've been able to peel away the layers of reticence I built up to protect my privacy. It is a testament to how far I have traveled since that sad day in Washington when I took stock that I can risk sharing my own experiences regarding weight loss and self-respect in the hope of helping others.

PART TWO

GEARING UP
TO TAKING OFF~
SOME
FAVORITE TIPS

CHAPTER ONE

Now that you've read my story, I'm sure you've realized that anyone can lose weight if really determined to do so. You saw how badly I let myself go, ballooning up to 180-odd pounds, and learned how I fought my way back. If I could win my battle to lose weight and regain my self-esteem you can too. In the end it comes down to real dedication and a lot of bloody hard work. Sure, there were plenty of times I got discouraged and wanted to give up, but each time I dug in my heels and said, "No, I'm not going to quit." And each time it got just a little bit easier.

Before describing my actual diet and exercise program I want to share the various hints and tips that helped me regain that twenty-two-inch waist. I'll never try and tell you dieting is fun. I know from painful experience just how tough taking off unwanted pounds can be, so in addition to the suggestions you are about to read, grab onto anything that will bolster your willpower and smooth the way. Whether it's psychiatry, saying your mantra, plotting your horoscope, casting runes or clutching a rabbit's foot, as long as it motivates you to succeed and isn't harmful to you or others, do it!

REWARDS TO KEEP YOU GOING

Even though only you can motivate yourself to lose weight, if anyone close to you offers bribes, take 'em! Once you've decided to diet, rewards from family and friends—as long as they are honestly well meant—can only help motivate you further.

Let me tell you about a young woman I met a couple of years ago. She was one of the most appealing girls I've ever known, with fair-haired, blue-eyed good looks. She was bright, vibrant and intelligent. She was also obese. She told me she was getting married in six months and was trying to lose weight. Although I normally don't go around poking my nose into other people's business, there are, as you know by now, occasions when I can't keep from interfering. On impulse, I handed this girl a mimeographed copy of my diet and said, "Follow this, and if you lose fifty pounds, I'll buy your wedding dress." You should have seen the expression on her face.

She took the diet home with her and for a few weeks was afraid to begin. She had been trying to slim down since she was a child. Her parents had taken her to nutritionists and clinics and special summer camps until she just couldn't bear to even hear the word "diet." She might never have started mine had her fiancé not stepped in. He told her at least to give it a try. She did. Later she told me it was the first time in her life she had actually enjoyed eating while on a weight-reduction plan.

By the time her wedding day rolled around she'd lost forty-five pounds. I still bought the dress. I wouldn't quibble over such a small number to go with such a large number already lost.

I can't say that the promise of the dress alone did the trick. But rewards do help. For me it was getting back into a pair of size-six jeans that I bought when I still weighed around 130. I adore wearing jeans, but they are just about the most revealing pants you can wear. Each week I would lie down on my bed and try to tug them on. After about month I could stand up in them. The only problem was that the zipper wouldn't close.

But the fact that I kept getting closer to my goal motivated me.

The other day I read something in the science section of the paper actually confirming my theories about rewards. Two mice were put in mazes. The first was given an easy course and lots of treats each time he completed the route, and he soon grew to enjoy his comfortable routine. The second was given a convoluted route, blocked every time he reached an exit, and given few pieces of cheese. After a few weeks both mice were dipped into a vat of water. And guess which mouse survived? Not the lean, well-exercised one. He gave up and drowned. It was the lazy mouse who kept struggling to get back to his happy life.

So make sure you give yourself lots of healthy rewards for starting on that diet and keeping at it.

ENCOURAGING WORDS

I'm also a great believer in the "encouraging word," especially when you're in an eating crisis. I know for a fact, when all else seems to fail, a thoughtful reminder from a loving friend can deliver you from temptation, whereas a rebuke or a snide crack does just the opposite. I know a very popular entertainer in her forties who has had a slight weight problem for years. She was one of those people who ate unthinkably. Hungry or no, if food was there, it went right to her mouth. Of course, it eventually wound up on her hips. She was married late in life to a man who adores her. About two years after their marriage, she developed high blood pressure and was told to lose weight. Her husband didn't care about her size but he did care about her health. He started commenting on what she was eating, not angrily but steadily. Naturally, she rebelled and told him to mind his own business. At his wit's end, he said, "Darling, I know I can't keep nagging you about your eating habits, so I've decided this will be my last word: The day your weight goes higher than your IQ, I'm leaving." She knew he didn't mean it, but the fact that he cared enough to worry about her health and was sensitive enough to phrase his concern in words he knew would make her smile has stopped her hand many a time on its way to the candy dish.

Here's another instance in which a simple phrase changed a friend's eating habits. She was taking a trip with a woman who apparently was shocked by the way my friend was wolfing down everything in sight. Later, when my friend complained she was gaining weight, her companion pointed out she was eating an awful lot of food. "But I can't help it," my friend said. "I just have to eat." Her companion answered very simply, "No, you don't. You can eat but you don't *have* to. Frankly, it's beneath your dignity to eat too much." For some reason that phrase stuck in my friend's mind. She later told me it made all the difference to her. Every time she was overcome with an insatiable lust for food, she'd say to herself, "It's beneath my dignity to eat too much," and it gave her the control she needed.

GETTING STARTED

You'll never lose weight if you never begin dieting. Unlike Scarlett O'Hara, you can't think in terms of to-morrow. Don't sit around waiting for the right phase of the moon or the first day of spring. Remember, procrastination kills inspiration. If you want to lose weight, begin now and make up your mind you'll give that diet a fair chance.

Don't sit around and think up excuses. Whether you're engaged in dieting or any other activity, "sitting around" is the biggest dodge of them all. There are women who spend most of the day on their butts, telephones clutched to their ears, discussing with friends what they are going to do and how they're going to do it. Somehow they never get around to doing anything. There are others whose chief activity is making luncheon appointments. While gobbling up the world's largest chef salad and all its caloric accoutrements, they talk *seriously* about getting down to the business of dieting. Weight loss is not attained in debate. Talk is really cheap when it comes to dieting. You have to spend each moment actively engaged in pursuing your intent. Lip service is a dis-service.

And unless you're one of the *rare* people with a bona fide medical condition, please refrain from using your thyroid as an excuse. It's an insult to your own intelli-gence as well as to those few unfortunates who do have an additional hurdle to overcome.

Sometimes I'm sure I've heard every excuse in the book to put off a diet. Or given it myself. People intent upon delaying really restricting their calories can justify the most flagrant overindulgence. How easy it is to trick ourselves into thinking we're doing everything we can to lose weight while we're actually stuffing ourselves. Do these phrases sound familiar? "I'm going to start a diet but we're having a big dinner at the club Saturday and we had to prepay." "There's a wedding next week, a Jewish wedding, and you know how great the food will be, so I'll start my diet right after." "I'm going to a spa next month, so I'll have to be on a diet then. I'll eat now because I'll be starving later." "I'm so worried about getting a job. I'll stop eating as soon as I'm employed." When will these people learn that any excuse is no ex-cuse?

I know a woman who for years has belonged to a nationally known weight-control group. She attends meetings every week, goes through all the group ther-apy, takes home all the printed information, fills her refrigerator with the prescribed green and leafy keys to diet success, and then proceeds to eat outside her house. The food rots in her icebox while she runs from pizza parlor to hamburger joint. Her defenses are such that you can't talk to her. Because she's a paying member of a weight-loss group, she's convinced herself that she's "dieting." Her behavior is completely contradictory. She walks into my house, barely says hello, and announces, "I'm hungry, what have you got to eat?" Next, she heads straight into the kitchen to check my refrigerator and cupboards. She actually berates me for not keeping sweets and starches! It's awful to watch but there's nothing anyone else can do about it. She has to want to change. I don't know how much longer she can continue to hide behind her membership card. I only hope, for her sake, she wakes up soon.

I have another friend who, for years, has religiously started a diet every Monday morning. She never makes appointments for that day. In fact, she doesn't go out socially until Wednesday. Monday and Tuesday she watches everything she eats and by Wednesday she'll call with the wonderful news that she's lost four pounds. Naturally, she wants to celebrate her success by eating, which she does for the rest of the week. By the time Sunday rolls around, she'll have put back the four pounds—plus. She dismisses her obvious gain by smiling and innocently announcing, "I can't understand why I don't fit in my clothes. I'll just have to start a diet tomorrow."

The moral of the story is, there is no point in gearing up to start if you don't plan to stick with it.

SET REASONABLE GOALS

Now that you're committed to losing weight make sure to set reasonable goals. Banish pipe dreams about your ideal weight. Just because you weighed 115 pounds at eighteen doesn't mean you should weigh the same at thirty-five. Pick a reasonable weight for your age and bone structure. You'll find you will be more relaxed and make a smoother adjustment to maintenance eating. Remember, when you diet, you are the only judge and jury. You have to answer only to yourself so ease up on the prosecution and hurry over to the defense.

Self-loathing does not provide good motivation. You can realize your potential and achieve what you want out of life only if you can forgive your weakness and accept yourself for what you are. In my mid-forties I was rich, famous, and was told by the media that I was beautiful. But I didn't accept myself and began on a self-defeating course of behavior. There was little joy or comfort in my life. Before I could set myself free from that unhappy and obese prison I had to learn to love myself all over again.

Another point to keep in mind is that how you look is more important than what you weigh. And it's just as important to be honest about looking good as it is to take off blinders about being obese. Your goal is to appear healthy and attractive. Since chances are you are not planning to audition as a stand-in for Twiggy, why pressure yourself with unrealistic images?

Suppose your ideal weight is 128, but when you reach 134 you actually look great. Stop there. The odds are that if you push to achieve too low a weight, the pounds will slip back no matter how carefully you watch what you eat.

I don't know why it is, but men seem much more at ease with their bodies than women. We always have nagging doubts. The most beautiful models often think they're not thin enough, and I've rarely met a woman who didn't want to lose a few pounds.

A friend of mine had the following experience. She went out to dinner with a man she had just begun dating. Impetuously he invited her to go to Catalina for the weekend. She immediately said no. It wasn't because she didn't want to, not at all. It was because the minute he mentioned Catalina, all she could think about was how horrible she would look in a bathing suit, how fat her thighs were, how much her stomach stuck out.

After about fifteen minutes of silently putting herself down, she looked at the man, who was easily twenty-five pounds overweight. It was clear he wasn't worrying about his appearance. In truth, he was probably happy with the way she looked, too. Otherwise he wouldn't have asked her to go. In the end she went and was happy she did.

All the time you are dieting, try to be happy with the weight loss you've achieved. Feel good about yourself and you'll find it easier and more enjoyable reaching your diet goals.

CHAPTER TWO

Now that you are in the right frame of mind it is almost time to get to the diet itself. You've made up your mind to begin, you've decided to ignore further excuses, you set yourself reasonable goals, and you are motivated by self-loving and not self-loathing. You know you deserve to look the best you can.

As you set off on the challenging road to looking great, here are a few more tips to make your diet easier while keeping you from slips or binges.

GET OUT THAT FULL-LENGTH MIRROR

Since self-honesty is essential to successful dieting, make sure that mirror is hanging in a place where you are able to view yourself without clothes. How many women look over the bathroom sink and judge their entire shape by the reflection in the medicine-cabinet mirror? Remember, I'm the lady who used to think she could see what she looked like in her compact. When you're trying to diet it's no time to play games. If you want lies, go to the circus and stand in front of the distorting mirrors. One of them can make you look ten feet tall and as narrow as a broomstick.

WRITE DOWN EVERYTHING YOU EAT

Some people do this religiously and it helps them. By keeping a written record they can't make excuses. Frankly, I don't need a notebook to remember what I've eaten. After all, it's my business to remember! I just apply my script-learning techniques. Don't scoff at recording your intake if you find it works for you. And don't cheat. If you walk down the street and eat a banana, you're eating a banana, not merely walking down the street.

By recording everything you eat, you can make your eating habits work for you. If you keep seeing entries at 4:00 P.M., then you can save a snack for that hour. Or if you notice you crave fruit just before you go to bed, plan to keep the apple or melon scheduled for dinner until then. A full record of your daily intake can be helpful in understanding your special needs. Sometimes when the food you're consuming is spelled out in front of you in black and white, it can shock you into taking action.

Don't, however, forget your manners and get carried away with the helpful procedure of taking notes. It's something that should be done surreptitiously or else it can become annoying.

Once, before I began dieting, I was at a formal dinner and I noticed that the woman across from me kept flipping open a small notebook after each course and studiously scribbling. Although I didn't recognize her, I assumed she was a reporter or a gossip columnist. Reporters always carry a notebook and you can spot them right away because they're continually jotting down names and information. That's okay for public appearances, I'm used to it, but this was supposed to be an intimate gathering and I was furious.

At the end of the evening, when I went to say good night I asked my hostess in my iciest tone why she hadn't told me she was inviting a reporter.

"Reporter?" she replied. "What reporter?"

"You know who I mean. That woman in the blue

dress who kept writing everything I said into her note-book."

"Oh, Elizabeth," laughed my friend. "Barbara's no reporter. She's just on a diet and she's supposed to write down everything she eats."

When you're dieting, be discreet. You don't have to report to your acquaintances as though they were the commanding officers of your Great War Against Fat. Even your most supportive friends can become bored. How do you know whether or not you are obsessing and talking too much about your weight? Well, for one thing, if you walk into a room and everyone turns away, you might think about changing your topic of conversation.

But don't turn your silence into an excuse for being careless about those calories. If you don't feel like carrying about little notebooks, there are other methods of keeping track.

I have one friend who uses a small tape recorder. It's so tiny he can slip it in his pocket and turn it on without ever taking it out. This is okay but sometimes he forgets to turn it off and his friends have become a bit wary about confiding in him. It's too much like talking to the KGB. He's also had some problems with acquaintances who don't know about his diet. I mean, it's a bit spooky to hear someone announce into thin air: "Fruit cup . . . fresh orange, grapefruit sections, melon balls . . . veal chop, lean . . . beans, green . . ."

I have another friend who bought herself a PC just for dieting purposes. Her ten-year-old nephew taught her how to use it and she swears she lost ten pounds just trying to figure out the software. Now she's mastered the rudiments and is having the best time figuring out her calories and carbohydrates on the small screen.

I've also seen dieters use a special pocket calorie calculator. You can take it anywhere, and besides storing the caloric content of food you've eaten that day, it sounds an alarm if you go over your allotted amount. If you can afford it, it's worth looking into.

Whatever your method, until dieting has become a way of life for you, it is essential to note down exactly what you eat each day.

LOOK YOUR BEST WHILE LOSING

Everyone needs incentive to diet. Losing weight is not something you leap into with joy. It's a chore. There is a reward at the end when you reach your desired weight, but keeping your spirits up along the way is important. There are many ways to do this. One is by making yourself as attractive as possible no matter what your size.

Remember the Hans Christian Andersen tale of the ugly duckling who becomes the beautiful swan? I think most of us perceive the process of becoming thinner as analogous. We start out as ugly, and only when we have shed our pounds are we revealed to be beautiful. We *want* to start as toads and turn into princesses. We're fat. We look terrible. We diet. We look great. My question is, why wait?

I say, whatever size you're starting from, look the best you can from the first day you begin dieting. If you have no interest in your appearance, why on earth would you want to take on the burdensome task of slimming down? Present yourself as a potential swan from the very beginning. It will help keep you motivated if when you look in the mirror you see someone worthy of all your effort. It's also human to lose interest in your appearance when you're fat. But you've got to have a positive feeling about yourself while you're losing weight. So you're fat. That doesn't mean you have to look like a shlump.

I know plenty of big ladies who are positively glorious-looking. They may wear a size sixteen or eighteen, but they're always well groomed, neatly coiffed and radiantly glamorous. Yet many dieters will throw on anything as long as it's dark in color. Their philosophy is "I'm fat so it doesn't matter how I look." Rubbish. It always matters how you look.

In the past when I was plump, I still enjoyed dressing up. It wasn't until I became really despondent and grossly overweight that I stopped caring about my appearance.

Not long ago I heard a joke that went: What's the difference between the fat lady and the elephant? The answer: About a hundred pounds and a black dress.

Years ago, we were advised that fat people should never wear bright colors. A lot of heavy people still believe this. And if it wasn't depressing enough that fatties were forbidden reds and yellows and pinks, pants were simply out of the question. What nonsense. I think you should dress yourself with pride and interest even if you plan to start your diet only next week. Pay attention to your total appearance, not just the size of your waist.

Guard the assets you were blessed with like a miser. God and my Irish grandmother gave me a good complexion and good coloring, and while I can't take credit for my genes I will take full honors for preserving my natural assets. I don't use expensive lotions. I wash my face with a basic soap and just apply a good moisturizer.

Except when I had to portray exotics like Cleopatra or older women like Martha in *Who's Afraid of Virginia Woolf?* I use a minimum of makeup on screen and I always do my own. I like playing around with colors, but I don't consider my face a canvas upon which I'm supposed to pile layers of paint. This is even truer off screen. Most of the time I don't even use a foundation. As I've gotten older, I've found glittery eye shadow and bright rouge tend to emphasize my age. The powders stick in the natural wrinkles, particularly around the eyes. So the more powder you use, the more you're accentuating what you're trying to disguise. The older you get, the more subtle you must be with your makeup. You have to accept yourself for what you are. If what you are includes some gray hairs and a few wrinkles, so what! Remember, self-acceptance is essential to many things and that includes a successful weight loss.

KEEP YOUR SENSE OF HUMOR

Try not to take yourself too seriously. We all know the jolly fat lady who's crying on the inside, but the well-disciplined dieter may find a hearty laugh at her own expense is just what she needs to keep her spirits up while she sticks to her goals.

I've always enjoyed a good joke and these days my outlook on life is generally optimistic. Just two years ago I made a television movie with my old friend Robert Wagner called *There Must Be a Pony*. The title is taken from a story Bob's character tells.

"You know the old joke about the man who had twin sons? One was an incurable pessimist, the other an incurable optimist. The father was stumped, so he tried an experiment on Christmas Eve. He put the pessimist in a room with everything a kid could wish for. And he filled the optimist's room with horse manure.

"Then he looked in on them to see how they were doing. The pessimist sat there in the middle of the toys and clothes and sporting goods—just sat there staring at everything suspiciously, trying to figure what the catch was. Then he went to the optimist's room and peeked in. There was the other boy, standing waist-high in all that manure, shoveling it over his shoulder, laughing. . . .

" 'Hey,' the father said. 'What are you so happy about?' The kid turned to him and said, 'Well, Dad, I figure with all this crap, there must be a pony!' "

Optimism really is its own reward, and it's an enormous asset when confronting the rigors of a diet.

Working on this movie with R.J. in 1986 was rewarding in many ways. It was the first time we had ever done a film together and it was the first time R.J. had seen me in person since I had lost all that weight.

In fact, this occasion was momentous in a few ways. When I walked on the set, R.J.'s jaw dropped. "My God, Elizabeth," he said, "you look wonderful!" It is a fabulous feeling to elicit such praise, and the great thing is, *anybody* who sticks to a diet can look forward to equally enthusiastic comments.

When R.J. had finished gasping, I asked him how he stayed so handsome and trim.

"Fear," he answered without a second's hesitation. "If I don't stay in shape, no one will hire me."

Even when I'm working I try to liven things up a bit with a prank or two. The thing I hate most getting ready for a movie is the costume fitting. It's a drag so I invent little mischiefs to amuse myself.

Not so very long ago, after a series of particularly long and involved fittings, one of Nolan Miller's young assistants was sent to my house to do some emergency adjusting. Everyone had been under a lot of tension about getting the costumes right, and as the girl worked, she told me that Nolan and his staff were afraid that I might lose my temper because of this last-minute work. I told her I wasn't cross, but it would serve them right if we played a joke on the famous designer.

After the girl finished, I went into my dressing room, got out a dark purple lipstick, and painted a perfect shiner on her right eye. Westmore would have been proud of me. It really looked as though she'd been belted.

She returned to Nolan's shop and burst in the door sobbing. "I'm never going up to that woman's house again!" The staff clustered around her. When she lifted her head they saw the blackened eye and she told them I had lashed out at her with my fist. They were furious and Nolan himself was taken in for a time. When the girl finally revealed the trick, everyone had a good chuckle and all of the pressure was eased.

Afterward Nolan said, "You know, Elizabeth, I've finally figured out what makes it work for you. It's your sense of humor. You can really laugh at yourself."

I think there's a lot of truth in Nolan's assessment. One of my strengths has been not taking myself, or my image, too seriously.

Certainly, without a sense of humor I would never have used one of my most effective diet tricks. Someone told me that Debbie Reynolds kept a photograph of me taken during my fattest period on her refrigerator door. She said it reminded her of what could happen if she charged into the icebox. During the initial stage of my diet I thought, well, if it works for Debbie, maybe it will work for me. I stuck a picture of myself at my worst on the refrigerator, and every time I went to the kitchen, there was my corpulent self reminding me what would happen if I broke my diet. That sight was an excellent deterrent to bingeing. If you think a picture of me as Miss Lard will inspire you, go ahead and put it on your refrigerator, I have no objection. Certainly there are enough photographs to choose from. I didn't exactly skulk about in those days, and even if I had tried to avoid the press, they would have found me.

Am I ashamed of how I looked at my heaviest? Well I'm certainly not proud, but to tell the truth, when I look at those pictures I feel more sadness than shame. Not so long ago I came across a photo taken back in Washington and what struck me most was not my size, but my hair, which fell in limp strands around my face. It's obvious to me now that by allowing myself to appear like that in public, I had stopped caring. Even more amazing, how could I have believed those Halston outfits really made me look slender? No matter how cleverly designed, no clothes could hide the bulk I was carrying. Confronting a picture of myself at my worst definitely helped keep that refrigerator door closed. It was a good ploy, and perhaps better than using a photograph of me, you might try putting up a picture of yourself.

Or you might try the little mechanical device a friend of mine attached in her refrigerator. Every time she opened the door a voice would call out, "Are you here again, Fatso?"

AVOID TEMPTATION

"I can resist anything but temptation," is a familiar quote, and the enticements a dieter faces are staggering. Television, magazines, billboards are always advertising delicious snacks. We aren't allowed to forget food for an instant and one of the most dangerous lures of advertising is to persuade us that other leisure activities are incomplete without something to eat: hot dogs at baseball games, nibbles in front of the TV, beer and colas between tennis sets. Then look what happens when we go downtown. You'd have to be made of steel to walk through a shopping mall without wanting to snack, when every other store is hawking ice cream, Chinese food, nuts and pizza. Your best protection here is to arrive right after breakfast or lunch, when your stomach is full, or to stop for a planned meal at one of the health stores.

Then take our time-honored ritual of going to the movies. It's never the simple action of buying a ticket. We've all been trained to load up on candy and popcorn. Here in Los Angeles there's an alarming trend toward expanding lobby menus. It's now possible to buy nachos, tacos, burritos, cookies, cakes and ice cream sundaes. The moviegoer has to run a gauntlet of goodies before taking a seat. Although it's best to learn to forgo the kind of automatic munching that accompanies other activities, if you know you can't sit through a film without moving your jaw, bring the right kind of food to the theater. I know one woman who takes a cellophane bag full of lettuce leaves. She finds she is content to crunch greens rather than kernels.

During one of my early visits to a spa, several of the women and I always brought special diet snacks with us to the movies. We'd scoot past the food counter and bitch about the smell of buttery popcorn, but keep our mouths busy with celery or carrot sticks. I swear I never thought I could walk past the popcorn machine at a movie theater. But I can and you can too. Again, it's a matter of pride. Good God, none of us is so weak that we're going to let a piece of popcorn defeat us. Actually, popcorn can be healthy snack, but not when doused in butter and salt as it usually is in the theaters.

At the outset of any diet it is generally wise to stay away from situations where you may be tempted to overeat. When you dine at friends' houses, most are willing to dish up skinless barbecued chicken and salads. But there are exceptions and you must be on guard.

Even today there are certain foods I simply avoid, like rolls and butter. It's so easy to finish two or three before dinner is served. If I'm going to blow calories, I'd rather do it on something I absolutely adore than on something I'm absentmindedly nibbling. As far as little tricks like breaking off a bit of bread or taking a spoonful of dessert, I cannot do those things when I'm dieting and I don't advise you to try either. I feel it's just teasing yourself. In the same way an alcoholic can never become a social drinker, a compulsive eater has to stay away from obvious perils. One sip, one taste, either can be equally dangerous for the respective addict. If you have a serious weight problem, I think you have to treat your obesity like an addictive disease. Fattening foods should be cut out of your diet because they're injurious to your health, and you should avoid anything that triggers your appetite.

An actress friend of mine has a novel approach to avoiding temptation. She classifies foods into two categories: "enemies" and "friends." The former are the calorie-laden goodies, the latter consist of sensible, nutritious fare. Whenever she sits down to a meal her aim is to surround herself with "friends." Anytime she gets into a situation where fattening foods are present, she immediately issues a battle cry. I actually heard her do it on a TV talk show. The host had a box of chocolates on his desk and he offered some to her. She threw up her hands and said, "Get them away! Those are my enemies." It's fun to watch her ward off the invading forces. "Listen," she told me. "If declaring war on fattening foods keeps me from eating them, I'm willing to fight." One time I saw her and she'd put on a few pounds. I didn't say anything. She sheepishly admitted, "I was taken prisoner by the enemy and brainwashed, but I'm breaking out soon." The next time I saw her, she had indeed made good her escape. Her approach may be far-fetched, but it works for her. Furthermore, children

Roddy was always able to capture my thoughtful moments.
(Photograph by Roddy McDowall)

ABOVE

First day of rehearsal for the Broadway production of *The Little Foxes;* an evening at the Academy Awards dinner; another photograph, from my fortieth birthday celebration; "into every woman's life, a little diamond should fall." *(Left to right, top: © Martha Swope; Ron Galella/Ron Galella, Ltd.; bottom: Norman Parkinson © 1972; Norman Parkinson © 1977)*

OPPOSITE PAGE

In my pre-caftan days. I wasn't afraid to wear white.
(Ron Galella/Ron Galella, Ltd.)

...Drinking
(© Felice Quinto)

...eating
(Rudolf Meidl)

...and gaining weight!
(Ron Galella/Ron Galella, Ltd.)

"Round and firm and fully packed, I crown
the Shenandoah Apple Blossom Queen."
(WINCHESTER STAR)

More ...and more weight!

(Top: Ron Galella/Ron Galella, Ltd.)

An example of the loss of self-esteem. I did not care
about my hair, my makeup, or my weight (*left*). This is
the photograph that I keep on my refrigerator (*right*).
(*Left: Jean-Paul Dousset/Agence Angeli;
right: courtesy of Liz Smith*)

The result of too much booze, food, pills, and no "click."
(*Jimmy Lowe*)

Acting with Geraldine Chaplin in *The Mirror Crack'd*.
My eyes, my face, my being reflect my own unhappiness.
(Weintraub Entertainments)

With Anthony Zerbe in *The Little Foxes*. That's tea in
my stage "wineglass." It was replaced with the real
stuff when the curtain fell.
(© 1985 Martha Swope)

Chatting with Richard, Rudolf Nureyev, and Tessa
Kennedy at my fiftieth birthday celebration in London.
(Doug McKenzie of PPS)

ABOVE

The immortal Martha Graham,
the fabulous Liza Minnelli, and I.
(David McGough/DMI)

OPPOSITE PAGE

Richard and I with Joan Kennedy at the
Boston preview of *Private Lives*.
(David McGough/DMI)

Victor Luna and I at the opening-night party
for *Private Lives*—ready to be plucked!!!
(David McGough/DMI)

are often taught to play games with food to make them eat. "Here comes the choo-choo into the tunnel." "Here comes the airplane into the hangar." "Here comes the automobile into the garage." These phrases are heard around high chairs everywhere. Well, why not turn them around? Silly, yes, but if it's effective, who cares?

Another good way to withstand temptation is by waiting it out. Again, you can apply some of the principles of AA. When a recovering alcoholic gets a craving for a drink, instead of going to the bar and pouring a shot, he stops and thinks rather than acts. "Okay," he says to himself, "I'll control myself for a minute." When that minute has passed, he says, "Okay, I made it for that minute, I'll try for another five." Dieters can use the very same technique, and when five minutes pass and you see you haven't dissolved into a puddle of shakes, you can say, "Well, I won't have it now. Maybe I'll have it tonight." When evening comes and the urge becomes unbearable, you go through the process again. The AA theory is based on one day at a time. If you apply this to overeating, the results should be equally successful. They are for me.

When I get an urge, it's usually for something like Tofutti, which, though healthier and lower in calories than ice cream, still has to be resisted if it's a day when I'm trying to diet. At such times I'll say to myself, "Wait a bit." Immediate gratification is for babies. I've actually gotten to the point where I know if I say "Wait," I'll wait until I finally skip the indulgence altogether for that twenty-four hours.

Another AA hint that can help when you become fixated on almond chocolate, deep-dish pizza or whatever no-no you crave is "Move a muscle, change a thought." This means that instead of sitting around and mooning about banana splits, why not read a book, go to the zoo, visit a museum, go dancing. Do anything that keeps your mind busy with thoughts other than calories. Sometimes the best distraction is to do something nice for someone you love, especially if that someone is yourself.

You should also be aware of what you're eating, particularly when temptations are put before you willy-nilly. Watch how other people approach a high-calorie meal. Many eat without thinking. A dish is put in front of them, they pick up the silverware, and off they go on a relatively uninterrupted roll till their plate is clean. They probably have no idea how much they have eaten. Even when I ate an awful lot, I didn't automatically jam food into my mouth. I take small bites and enjoy the flavor. It's a good habit I learned in my childhood. I'm amazed at the number of people who literally shovel the food in without even tasting it. At least when I was pigging out I savored every mouthful.

I also never fell into the trap of sneaky eating. I ate a lot but never on the sly. Some fat people will only pick at their food in public. Whenever I went out with a certain friend of mine she would never touch the bread or rolls, would order sensible entrées, and would never ask for any dessert except fruit. Meanwhile, she weighed over 200 pounds. For a long time, I bought the story that her metabolism was so screwed up she couldn't lose weight no matter what. Maybe not, but one night after a dinner party at her house, I saw what she really ate.

She had cleared the dishes into the kitchen and after she'd been absent for a while I decided to go and see if I could help with anything. I found her standing over the sink scraping the plates. But before she threw away the scraps, she was shoving the choice pieces into her mouth. I felt so sorry for her. All the time she was blaming her metabolism, she had to live with this monumental lust. I ducked away before she saw me, but I have never forgotten the sight of her putting garbage into her mouth. I was a human garbage disposal but never on the sly and never with anyone else's food.

Another trick to control the speed with which you eat is to look over your plate carefully before you begin. Not only will this give you the pleasure of regarding the contents, it will give you the opportunity to gauge the amount and decide how much you're actually going to consume.

Don't fall into the trap of feeling you can't leave food on your plate. When you dine out, someone may put half a chicken on your plate. You don't have to finish it. This was a hard lesson for me to learn. Like most of my generation, my brother and I were constantly told, "Eat everything. Children are starving in China." (Lauren Bacall tells a story about her son Stephen who, when given the same warning, looked up and said, "Name two.") If you wish to help people who are less fortunate, raise money to send food. Don't worry about what's already been cooked and served.

PRESENT YOUR FOOD ATTRACTIVELY

Just because you are putting controlled portions on your dinner plate, there is no reason that plate can't be arranged to look both full and attractive. If you can't indulge your appetite you can feed your other senses. By this I mean that even if you have only one lamb chop for dinner, why not serve it in the most elegant manner possible? Use your best china or designate some dish you particularly admire just for your own use. Every spa understands the importance of presentation. One of the fanciest treats its clients to delicate lace place mats, double damask napkins, crystal water goblets, magnificent silverplate and real porcelain plates. Fresh-cut flowers grace every table. Even if you cannot afford such a service, you can please your eye with pretty pottery and a single daisy or petunia in a jelly jar. As long as it's just for *your* use and *your* pleasure, it will make a difference.

If you're a homemaker and have a husband and kids to look after, you know what a luxury it is to be able to do something just for yourself. Remember, to diet successfully it's important to express self-love in constructive, caring ways.

DIET FOOD CAN TASTE DELICIOUS

There's absolutely no reason for you to eat food that is tasteless and uninteresting. Yes, portions have to be limited, but you don't have to insult your taste buds. A diet may be boring but it doesn't have to be bland. There are so many nonfattening condiments and spreads to perk up flavor. Many can be found in your local market, but there are also speciality stores that carry unique items that add excitement to low-calorie dishes. I recommend you spend some time browsing through health-food stores. Not only will you find foods that are specially prepared for healthy eating, you'll find lots of ways to vary the taste of diet meals. If the difference between the flavor of a product you like and one you don't is only two calories, go ahead, indulge yourself. Just don't overindulge. Once you progress to maintenance, you find even more products that are real godsends. I now enjoy a fourteen-calorie fruit jam on my breakfast toast. And there are several diet mayonnaises that have only forty calories a tablespoon. (I actually prefer to whip up my own dressing, but I'll keep the other in the refrigerator for emergencies.)

It is also worth testing the various salt substitutes on the market as well as the flavorful condiments created from dried vegetables. And remember, regular herbs and spices are generally almost without calorie content, and ocean salt used sparingly is much better for you. Dieters are lucky to be living in an age when they can purchase such ingredients from all over the world. Sometimes, the more exotic the herb the more exciting the meal, though not all spices appeal to everyone. I think coriander, or cilantro, imparts a fabulous taste, but I have a friend who insists it tastes like soap. Several foreign cuisines that have become popular in the United States are known for being a dieter's boon. Notably Chinese, Japanese and, more recently, Thai. When dining out on these foods do check the ingredients and methods of cooking. Such dishes as sweet-and-sour are not only fried but also dipped in batter and heavy in sugar content. Still, most Oriental dishes are prepared in just a bit of oil, and wok cooking can be a great dieter's aid when eating out or at home. And don't overlook steaming, either. Steamer baskets are sold everywhere and it's extremely simple to prepare vegetables in them. Because steaming preserves the moisture and freshness, you don't have to use butter or oil. A sprinkling of herbs or spices over the ingredients ensures a tasty, nutritional dish.

I love to experiment with food and my ingenuity is really put to the test when I'm trying to lose weight. In the last few years I've come up with a number of amazingly good substitutes, particularly in desserts, where a little sweetener can go a long way. The man who invented Tofutti spent years before he finally created a really terrific ice cream alternative. Though I wish someone would invent a low-cal version of my favorite *crème brûlée,* I'll console myself in the meantime with Tofutti and frozen yogurt.

Keep yourself from feeling deprived and you won't get depressed. I don't mind spending time making things good for me. If you don't think you're worth the bother, then you've got trouble with your self-worth.

Surprise yourself! Surprise your taste buds. Keep them amused and your stomach will have less to bellyache about.

LEARNING TO EAT WITH NON-DIETERS

Although you may wish to avoid restaurants and dinner parties—as I did—on the first few weeks of your diet, it is both impossible and unwise to dine in solitary splendor for more than a short time, and if you are surrounded by a slender and hungry family, you have to face dieting in the face of temptation from the word go. Worst of all, you may find yourself chewing greens opposite one of those lucky skinnies who never gain no matter how they gorge themselves.

In time I learned to dine out with pleasure even when cutting calories. For one thing, I knew I had no choice. Just as an alcoholic must learn to move around in a society where others are drinking, so must a foodoholic be able to dine with those whose diet is not restricted.

At the beginning of my diet I turned down a number

of wonderful invitations just because I was afraid I wouldn't be able to control myself. When I finally broke down and accepted a dinner engagement I was more nervous about what I was going to eat than what I was going to wear. I finally chose a dress so tight that I couldn't have eaten an extra lettuce leaf! It was pretty uncomfortable but it got me through the evening.

Eventually I learned to take an ornery kind of pleasure in denying myself in the midst of plenty. If you're on a diet and doing well, rub it in. Be outrageously virtuous and let your exaggerated behavior act as a shield. Pass up the wrong foods as though they were stepping stones to hell and let the "no thank yous" fall like rain.

This brings up a relevant question. When at home, no matter what your family's previous snacking habits, why have fattening foods around at all? Take advantage of your own dieting to help establish good eating habits for your family, even the skinnies. Try cleaning out the cookies and potato chips and replacing them with nutritious and tasty substitutes. Teaching your family how to eat properly is a splendid pursuit. They don't have to diet, just avoid that calorie-laden junk. For example, if you're making potato skins for yourself, you can give them whole baked potatoes, and believe me, they will never know whether you are sautéeing their chicken in a little unsaturated oil or half a stick of butter.

Whatever you do, get those you live with to help. Sit the family down and level with them. Tell them you're concerned about your weight and that you have to watch what you eat. You'd be amazed at how supportive the people who love you can be . . . *if* you give them the chance. I was never a sneaky dieter any more than I was a sneaky eater. Once I stopped talking about dieting and began doing it, everyone around me tried to be helpful. One friend commented later on how amazed she was when we were on the phone one day and I said, "I have to go now. I'm eating lunch." She said that's when she knew I was going to make it. Before, I would eat while

I talked. Today I wouldn't consider doing that. In fact, I find it annoying when I'm speaking to someone over the telephone and I can hear chewing.

Although my family was generally supportive of my efforts to stick to my diet, we all know that unfortunate spouse or acquaintance who, whether consciously or not, pushes the forbidden. Just as the alcoholic is urged to try "one little drink" so is the dieter urged to take "one bite." We all know people like this, and though they profess to be friends, I think their behavior is thoughtless and mean-spirited. Learn to deal with those who say, "Oh, you look wonderful, have another piece of cake." Or, "Gee, you look great, but how can you refuse my lasagna? I made it just for you and it's really low in calories." Be on guard for remarks like "Have another piece" or the classic "Just this once." Sometimes when people nag at me about what I should eat, I turn the tables and ask them to describe to me what they're eating: "Tell me, how does it taste? What's the consistency? Describe the texture. Does it just sort of slide down your throat? How intense is that chocolate, anyway?" Enough questions and the person tends to leave you alone. It's perverse, but it works!

Today my dining pattern is so firmly established my friends try not to let me break it even when I want to. Last year I went out for dinner with a dear pal who had been a frequent dinner companion during my diet. We went with another couple to a restaurant on Santa Monica Boulevard, and when the waiter came over, my friend began to order for me, saying, "Miss Taylor will have the broiled fish, steamed vegetables, and lettuce and toma—" I interrupted him in mid-sentence. "No I won't, I'll have the sirloin steak, mashed potatoes, peas, and mixed salad with Russian dressing on the side." My friend turned to me with his mouth open and said, "Elizabeth, what are you doing?" I laughed and spent the rest of the meal reassuring him that every once in a while it was okay for me to eat what I wanted.

I know that I would never have been able to lose weight as successfully as I did without the help of my friends. Should your friends not be equally understanding and supportive, they may not be your friends.

PLATEAUS

No matter what support systems you set up, they are rarely strong enough to keep you from getting discouraged during those inevitable stretches when you continue to diet rigorously but fail to lose. What could be worse than getting on the scale, possibly for several weeks in a row, and seeing the marker steadfastly cling to a single number. I know, I've been there.

When I started my diet, I was advised by a doctor not to weigh myself every day. He said to get on the scale once a week to avoid as much as possible the negative feedback of sitting on a plateau. Would I listen? Of course not. I wanted to plot each day's descent, like a reverse Dow Jones. That was fine until I hit the first of my plateaus. Every day I stepped on the scale and weighed exactly what I had the day before. After a week I stared at the numbers in disbelief, waiting for the indicator to assure me there had been an error. There hadn't. I desperately wanted to find an excuse, but I had no clothes to remove and, though my hair was still damp from the shower, I couldn't convince myself that the moisture counted. I got off the scale and quickly leaped back on with both feet. I hoped that an equal distribution of weight would manifest itself in a lower number. Alas, the jump approach didn't help either. If anything, the indicator seemed to move up a hair. No amount of juggling on my part would sink that needle. Only someone who's been through this kind of ordeal can fully appreciate the gloom of the stalled dieter.

Don't suffer in silence. Tell your friends you need their encouragement. Have them help you plan enjoyable activities to pass the time until the weight begins to melt again. More important, be very good to yourself. It will take all your willpower not to say, "I'm not losing anyway, so why should I deprive myself?" Visions of renounced meals will appear in your head until you're ready to march to the table and make up for lost time. Don't! Dig in your heels and try to ease that feeling of deprivation with nonedible treats. This is a perfect time to try a new hairstyle, indulge in a facial, or buy a new dress. Do whatever you need to do to stick it out for as long as it's necessary to break that plateau. Even if it takes several weeks, you will eventually see results. So don't give in and don't give up.

THE PIG-OUT

Once you have reached your first reasonable diet goal and are not trapped on a plateau, you can indulge in one of the most rewarding features of my particular diet—the controlled pig-out. This is designed to let you indulge in your favorite foods without breaking the diet or maintenance regime.

Once a week, and for one meal only, you can yield to your wildest food fantasies and eat whatever you please. There is no harm in such indulgence as long as you're prepared to return to your diet immediately afterward.

My splurges usually consisted of fried chicken, mashed potatoes and gravy, and cornbread. I've also eaten an entire pizza, followed by a hot fudge sundae. The point is, you can have anything your heart desires, *but* at the very next meal you must be back in control.

I think it's a good idea to pig out on the same day each week. I used to do it on Saturday night or Sunday lunch. I don't recommend doing it on the last day of one week and the first day of the next. It's too unbalanced. And don't forget it's just *one* meal. And it's probably best to schedule your pig-out for midday rather than evening. That way you'll have more time to work it off and you won't go to bed feeling bloated.

I had my first pig-out when I reached 132 pounds. I dreamed about it all the way down from 160 pounds. Over and over in my mind I served and savored that meal. While I was actually eating six ounces of skinless white chicken meat and veggies, I fantasized about a huge fried chicken leg, coated with breaded skin, resting on a gravied mountain of mashed potatoes.

Once in a while, if I wanted a little variation to my dream, I'd substitute my childhood favorite—Devonshire clotted cream. Aside from a passion for this delicacy, one fortunate habit I learned growing up in England was to expect smaller portions than are usually served in the States. My brother and I were also not brought up to expect food rewards. We were given cake for tea or supper, but not as a treat for finishing a task or being on our best behavior. I don't think the British children I knew when I was little would understand the pig-out, but I don't know too many Americans who would not.

These days I tend to eat more normally and I can eat a fattening meal on occasion without worrying. Sometimes weeks will go by without my having a pig-out. But when I do it can be memorable. One of the best I remember was in London in August 1986. George Hamilton and I had just flown in, and by the time he had finished his business and come by the Dorchester Hotel to take me to dinner, I was tired and unusually cranky. I'd originally planned to stay at a friend's house, but the press had found out and made such a commotion it seemed wiser to change my plans. Consequently, instead of being able to spend a week relaxing in private I was confronted with all the hullabaloo of a hotel visit. Worse, yet, when George and I reached the dining room it was closed.

We went back to the room and asked the operator if we could get a hot meal from room service. Time passed and we were really getting hungry. Neither of us had eaten anything since leaving the plane.

"What happened to the operator?" I asked.

"We'd better check," said George. He called back and asked what was going on. The operator apologized for the delay. It seems the chef had gone home to bed and they had to waken him to get him back. He had just that moment returned. George took the receiver away from his face and smilingly told me the story.

"What would you like to order, Elizabeth, Dover sole?"

It was now about one o'clock in the morning, but I was in England, I wanted to eat a great English dinner.

"No, George. I want roast beef, Yorkshire pudding, mashed potatoes with gravy, and pudding with Devonshire cream!"

George gave the order, and around quarter of two, a waiter called up and said that dinner was ready. The chef wanted to know if we wished him to come up and carve. I said it was very sweet, and we'd like to thank him for his trouble, but he didn't have to come in person unless he wanted to. Ten minutes later, our meal was wheeled into the room, followed by the chef who was dressed in spotless whites, a starched toque on his head. He bowed courteously and proceeded to carve the roast and serve the dinner. Everything on the cart had been prepared from scratch—and just for the two of us. And what a meal it was, right down to the extravagant dessert—a luscious *crème brûlée* stuffed with peaches and topped with the thinnest crispest layer of brown sugar imaginable. Though the chef had his head down as he went about his work, both George and I thought he looked familiar—and indeed he should have. Our culinary benefactor was Anton Mosimann, one of the most famous chefs in the world. I will never forget that dinner, and I count it among the most memorable and serendipitous experiences of my life.

One of the great benefits of having maintained my weight for over three years was that I was able to eat pretty much whatever I wanted that whole trip. In fact, on the way back to L.A. we were scheduled to stop in Washington and I called John Warner just before we took off. "Hello, John, we'll be at Dulles International for several hours tomorrow and would love to see you. It would be great if you'd come to the airport and visit. And maybe bring some leftover fried chicken. You do have some fried chicken around, don't you?" John laughed, "Don't worry, honey, I'll be there to see you . . . with the chicken."

John went into the garden, picked some fresh ears of corn, fried up some chicken himself, and when we arrived at Dulles was waiting there with a packed lunch! We had a lovely time, and on the second lap of the journey, from Washington to L.A., George and I feasted on our "catered" meal.

The next day when I got on my scale, I discovered I'd actually lost four pounds. I must have burned them up in energy.

Part of the joy of being slim for several years is the ability to take a vacation from counting calories and carbohydrates. But you can do this only when you have maintained an ideal weight and been in control of eating habits for a long time.

BINGES

Bingeing is totally different from the controlled pig-out. Whether you are on your diet or even have reached your desired weight and are on maintenance, you really can't afford to set aside proper eating patterns for a prolonged period of time. If you do, the weight will creep right back on and you will have trouble ending that old yo-yo syndrome. Remember how I kept gaining and losing the same fifteen pounds for a while?

Lapses can begin insidiously, so a dieter must be on National Guard duty twenty-four hours a day, three hundred sixty-five days a year. And whenever you have a question about your appearance, remember the mirror or, as in my case, those tight-fitting jeans. There's no way to lie to your image.

One of the reasons I strive to be a couple of pounds under my ideal weight is so that small slips don't lead to disaster. I've slipped and almost let leeway become a freeway back to fat. A few years ago, I was hospitalized because of my back. I was in for three months and put on many, many pounds. It took a while to get them off, but I did. George Hamilton actually thought that period of time marked my "heaviest." Then I showed him the old photos, the ones from my 180-pound–plus days. He couldn't believe it! You can't relax your regimen. More recently I was hospitalized for oral surgery and put on a liquid diet. You'd think that would ensure my losing weight but *liquid* is a pretty broad term and covers selections like frappés, milk shakes, malteds and that delightful New York City creation, the egg cream. On this "restricted" diet, I really junked on ice cream, only I managed to block what I was doing from my consciousness. I innocently sipped my way up the scale and might have floated up even further had I not caught sight of myself in the ubiquitous full-length mirror when I returned home and was floating straight down the hallway toward the kitchen.

"Whoa, great white whale," I said to my image, noting the telltale bulge around the belt line. I immediately cut out the rich sodas and substituted vegetable and fruit juices. And when I was able to eat solid foods again, I made sure they were properly nourishing and not merely filling.

One of the great dangers of a lapse is that it can trigger a prolonged binge. You've adhered to your regimen for four weeks, lost up to eleven pounds, and then one night you suddenly go berserk and wolf down a slice of chocolate cake. Your first thought is, the diet's over, you've lost control. To prove it, you may even eat another piece of cake or add some ice cream, a roll and butter, a candy bar, a beer to wash it down. As one piece of cake goes, so will the entire contents of the refrigerator, right down the gullet. There's an inevitable domino effect.

No, there isn't.

A lapse need not be a landslide. It escalates only if you let it. And you know what—even if you stuff your face for a week, that is not a signal that you are weak, incompetent and worthless. It also doesn't mean that you've failed and that your weight loss is over. You've simply had a setback, so stop thinking about what you just ate and start concentrating on what you didn't eat over the past weeks or months. Wasn't that *great,* and weren't you in control? You know you have the strength to go right back on your diet. You proved you can do it once and you can do it again.

After a while, you'll be happy to know, you'll lose

the desire to binge. Once your gastrointestinal tract has been treated to a steady diet of sensible food, it's liable to act up if you overload. Mine does. Last summer I went on a weekend cruise after a bout of blood poisoning. My friend's boat was docked nearby and we boarded early on a Friday morning. I was so washed out when breakfast was served, I thought I'd better eat a hearty one to get my strength up. Hearty it was, followed by an even heartier lunch. After the noon meal, my stomach started to churn. Poor little tummy, it was reacting to the unaccustomed sausages and ham, butter and croissants, omelets and scones. I spent the rest of the sail chewing antacids.

Get yourself past those inevitable binges and you'll find maintaining healthy eating habits becomes easier. Never doubt that you can do it, no matter how fat you are. If you need courage, turn to the pictures of me at my heaviest, or when I slipped. It can happen! Look at what I was and how I look today. If I could do it, so can you.

MAINTENANCE

You've dieted rigorously, avoided lapses or recovered quickly, and have achieved your ideal weight. Does this mean you can relax and eat anything you want? Unfortunately, no. Any dieter who resumes her old habits will soon find herself growing out of her new dress size.

All the time you are losing weight you should be teaching yourself patterns of eating and attitudes toward food to last the rest of your life. The key to successful dieting is keeping the weight off, but we often forget the importance of maintenance because the diet gets all the headlines.

Though you'll often hear the words "I'm on a diet," have you ever heard anyone proclaim, "I'm on maintenance eating"? Diet can offer the immediate gratification of weight loss. Maintenance can become monotonous.

What is maintenance, anyway? I think it's normal eating modified to the specifications of the individual. After the rigors of a strict regimen, you know very well which foods are dangerous. While you cannot spend the rest of your life giving undue attention to what you eat, you can remember the facts you learned while dieting and use them to modify your eating habits. For the rest of your life, you should classify foods into simple groups. In my own mind, when I look at food I automatically think, "Okay," "Take it easy" and "Better not." There's no question about calorie-laden items like rich desserts, but watch out that you gradually don't transform healthful salads and veggies with butter or heavy, calorie-laden dressings. The insidious ways we can return to weight-gaining patterns are terrifying.

One trick I learned the moment I started maintenance was either to take in or to give away the old sacks, pup tents and tarpaulins I used to conceal my bulk. I know I'll never again buy clothes with elastic waistbands. They're dangerous because they allow you to put on pounds and feel comfortable. Don't do it. One of the surest safeguards against gaining back the weight you've lost is dresses and skirts that pinch if you become too casual about what you eat.

All those who have struggled with their weight can never afford to drop their guard permanently. Though I've maintained my weight for almost three years, there have been a few occasions where I strayed from the slender and narrow—sometimes because of illness and other times because I was lulled into thinking I had everything licked. Me? I could handle food. After all, I'd sustained my loss beautifully. I began to think I was invincible and ate to prove it.

Once I went on a mini-binge just before I had to make a public appearance. Nolan Miller was making a dress for the occasion and I knew the waist would have to be eased. When you're wearing jersey, even a few pounds make a difference. I called and told him I had put on a bit of weight. "How much?" he asked. "Oh, about three pounds," I answered. There was a slight pause. "Elizabeth, is that a *real* three pounds or a theatrical three pounds?"

Actually, Nolan knows I'm as honest about my weight

as I am about my age, but the temptation is always to minimize those added pounds. Don't. Never confuse three pounds with ten. So keep up your guard, stay alert, and enjoy a lifetime of being slim, vibrant and healthy.

ONE LAST WORD

The diet that you are about to read, the one I used to take off all those pounds, is based on sound nutritional principles. It promises no miracles and no easy shortcuts. To diet means to regulate and if you are honestly interested in losing weight safely and permanently, you'll have to forget about the gimmick regimens that include ice cream, chocolate and even champagne in their titles.

Richard and I went on the Drinking Man's Diet after we made *Who's Afraid of Virginia Woolf?* It worked for a while and then we dropped the "diet" and just continued drinking. I can't think of a program worse for the liver.

Avoiding gimmicks does not mean starving or confining yourself to lettuce leaves and raisins. As far as I'm concerned, there is no reason to suffer hunger pangs. Though some diets promote the notion, why should you go hungry? Chances are you will only regain the weight once you return to normal eating.

Finally, be careful not to get carried away. Ironically, a compulsive eater easily can turn into a compulsive dieter—and that's dangerous. If you don't put on the brakes and play it smart, you can develop anorexia, and I wouldn't want anybody to use my diet as a springboard to disease. Make sure you go to maintenance eating the moment you've reached a sensibly thin weight. Too many women today trap themselves into starving or rely on maintaining their weight through bulimia.

I first heard about bulimia years ago. I was being treated by a New York doctor and noticed a young woman in his waiting room who was so pathetically thin it was pitiful to look at her. She was a famous model whose tragic story the doctor later told me. In order to maintain her slender figure, this woman ate and then put her finger down her throat. The horror was, she had been doing it for so long her system began to reject food automatically. She didn't have to make herself regurgitate, it had become a reflex. She could no longer hold down food even when she wanted to. The poor creature was admitted to the hospital and put on an intravenous drip. It was too late. She began hemorrhaging and shortly afterward died. She was barely thirty years old.

That was twenty years ago. Today, even though we've been made aware of the dangers of compulsive dieting, eating disorders have become more and more widespread and the victims are often touted as "ideals." There's a coterie of dames in New York City who make headlines because of their tiny waistlines. Newspaper columns and magazine articles chronicle their adventures and make it sound as though their lives are the epitome of glamour. Of course, no one mentions that each of them is either borderline or actually anorexic. One is known to suffer from bulimia. The manager of a thrift shop she patronizes reports that her donated apparel comes into his store reeking of vomit. Doesn't that sound glamorous?

These are extreme cases, to be sure, but they should serve as a warning. Remember, my diet is a sensible one and yours should be too.

PART
THREE

THE
TAYLOR~MADE
DIET

CHAPTER ONE

When my moment of truth arrived, I made up my mind that not only did I need to lose weight, I wanted to lose weight. I had the will but needed to find the way. There were dozens of diets to choose from. Friends recommended this or that best-selling book on the subject. I must have read them all, including a few that never made it to the top of the charts. I also boned up on nutrition and consulted with doctors and other weight-loss authorities. Still, I never found the perfect diet, the one magic formula that would help me lose weight without at the same time making me feel faint with hunger and generally deprived. Which is one reason why I never stayed on a diet for very long.

In the end, I improvised, discarding what seemed impractical, unhealthy or just plain boring, and putting the rest together in ways that made sense for me and the way I live. While my Taylor-made plan was designed to my specific needs and tastes, it is a nutritionally sound program. It should help anyone who wishes to lose weight the only way it can be successfully taken off—slowly and permanently.

Like any dieter I wanted to be instantly thin, yet I learned to be wary of diets that promised immediate, effortless results. You should be too. When and if such diets deliver on their promise of quick weight loss, they tend to be unhealthy and to leave you looking drawn and a good ten years older. Not only that, we now know that pounds lost in great haste are almost always regained with equal speed. Except for love at first sight and winning the lottery, there are very few legitimate instant miracles in the real world. A safe, sure, long-lasting weight loss is not among them.

If it took months or years to get fat, you can't realistically expect to regain your figure in a few short weeks. And you certainly can't expect to stay thin without making some permanent changes in your eating habits. Instant weight loss is not the key to my diet. Instead, the diet is planned to do something better: to help reeducate your appetite by supplying good, healthy food in portions small enough to keep you losing and large enough to keep you satisfied.

Which brings me to diet priority number two. No real deprivation. I knew that losing weight meant a commitment to months of dieting. I was willing to do that but I was determined to avoid feeling famished all the time. I could accept a certain amount of self-denial. (Isn't that what dieting is all about?) I knew I would have to trade the instant gratification of eating anything I wanted for the greater satisfaction of looking and feeling wonderful. But I wasn't prepared to deal with constant hunger. Life's too short to court misery, even for a good cause. Moreover, I was convinced it was possible to lose weight without undergoing that kind of agony.

As it turned out, I was right. With the help of Liz Thorburn, a talented chef, I worked out a series of low-fat, low-calorie menus that are practically hunger-proof. Although I must admit I occasionally craved my favorite foods, I never knew the pain of an empty stomach because the food on my diet is both filling and delicious.

Interesting food, appealing to the eye as well as the palate, is essential to everyone who plans to stay on a diet for more than a few days. Frankly, I can't think of a single reason why low-calorie meals should be boringly presented or lacking in variety, unless it's because the people who dream up the diets are so focused on calorie counts that they neglect to consider esthetics. As the

Japanese say, feast the eye before you feast the stomach. If beautifully presented, anything tastes better! Fancy health spas flourish because they care about the presentation as well as the nutrition of the meals they serve. In this respect, my diet really is different from the run-of-the-mill home programs. The dishes are creatively (though simply) prepared to make the most of every single calorie in terms of taste, texture and nutrition. And they're a joy to behold. You may be consuming fewer calories on my diet than you've been used to, but you'll savor every bite.

Since the diet was originally planned for my own use, it naturally includes many of my favorite dishes—crab salad, spicy chicken, crunchy Parmesan-flavored potato skins, and a variety of fresh fruit salads that you can dress up with Liz's fabulous low-cal mayonnaises. You'll also find a bit more lean steak and hamburger than you might expect on an ordinary diet. I love red meat. Despite its cholesterol content it can, in moderation, be part of any sensible diet. In fact, my favorite lunch is lean grilled hamburger on a slice of thin whole-wheat toast spread with a dab of peanut butter! However, on the day I eat it you can be sure that other cholesterol-rich foods are kept to a minimum.

One final word: Before going on this or any diet, be sure to consult your doctor. I can't imagine he or she will object to my regimen. It's nutritionally sound and allows a healthy amount of daily calories. Still, it's very important to get a medical checkup and your doctor's advice before starting any weight-loss program.

BASIC PRINCIPLES

Before we get to the diet itself, I want to explain a few dos and don'ts.

Don't look for daily calorie totals. You won't find them here, and not because I believe calories don't count. They do, but I'm convinced that weight loss depends more on enjoying modest amounts of highly nutritious, low-fat foods—with the emphasis on fruits, vegetables, chicken and seafood—than on playing a numbers game.

It's too easy to become fixated on calories, too tempting to say to yourself, "Ummm . . . I can have twenty potato chips for 230 calories, or six ounces of chicken for 310 calories." And then go for the potato chips. That's no way to lose weight.

If you must know the number of calories you will be getting on my diet, it's somewhere in the neighborhood of 1,000 a day. On the maintenance plan, the calories vary between 1,200 and 1,500 daily.

Breakfast. This always includes a serving of fruit, a slice of whole-wheat toast (dry) and your choice of tea or coffee. I won't insist that you drink your morning beverage black. Add a splash of low-fat milk if you like (it will add a little calcium, but very few calories). Artificial sweetener, which I use, is up to you.

For variety's sake, I prefer a different fresh fruit each morning. If the "fruit of the day" is out of season, or you're allergic to it, or you just don't like it, fine. The diet will work just as well if you have an orange, a piece of melon or a grapefruit every morning.

Lunch. Except on days when I indulge myself with lean grilled steak or hamburger, this meal almost always consists of a salad made with vegetables, fruit, chicken, seafood or other protein. What makes these salads special are the amazingly tasty low-calorie dressings. Whether it's a creamy vinaigrette, tangy blue-cheese or the special mayonnaise à la Liz Thorburn (recipe on page 207), each and every one is a flavorful improvement on the tired old squeeze of lemon juice called for on most diets. Of course, if you *prefer* lemon juice on your salads, go ahead and squeeze away. Keep in mind that when you are away from home at lunch you can easily prepare these salad-plus lunches before you leave and take them with you in plastic containers. Put the dressing in one container and the greens in another, and toss just before eating for a really fresh taste.

Some days when I have morning-to-evening fittings or back-to-back interviews, I find it more convenient to drink my midday meal. This is particularly true when I'm filming and I don't want to take the time or trouble to redo my makeup after eating. At such times my old Hollywood training comes in handy. In those days my costumes were either so tight or so expensive I couldn't eat a normal meal. I had to lean against a slant board and sip nourishment through a straw. For those dieters who also may wish a liquid lunch alternative, I have included this option: a protein powder drink that you can make according to instructions on the container or turn into a fabulous low-cal "malted milk" with the recipe on page 194. Needless to say, liquid protein lunches, too, can be prepared ahead and stored in a Thermos bottle. And if you don't have to worry about your makeup, you can include a few raw vegetables and a couple of low-calorie crackers to add crunch.

Mid-afternoon snack. I mentioned earlier that I'm rarely hungry on my diet, but when hunger does strike, it's usually sometime between lunch and dinner. That's when a snack can save the day. My favorite, because I can eat and eat and still feel virtuous, is a big plate of assorted raw vegetables, or crudités, served with one of Liz's dips or vinaigrettes.

Dinner. This meal always includes fish, shellfish, chicken or, more rarely, red meat, accompanied by green, yellow or red vegetables. I also allow myself a small serving of starch, half a cup of rice perhaps, or a few new potatoes. Believe me, many of the meals are elegant enough for entertaining. Your guests won't even suspect the dishes are dietetic. Recipes and suggestions for sauces and seasonings can be found beginning on page 203.

Whether or not you want to fuss over the meal is entirely up to you. When in doubt, in a hurry or just plain too tired to make a production out of dinner, simply broil or grill fish, chicken or meat; steam the vegetables or serve them raw. Sauced or simplified, the nutrition is the same and the difference in calories almost nonexistent. You'll lose weight either way, which of course is what this diet is all about.

Substitution. Just as it isn't necessary to cook the food on my diet exactly as called for in the recipes, as long as you don't add extra butter, oils or other calories, you can also substitute items of similar nutritional and caloric value. For example, we all know steak has no magical diet properties; lean hamburger will do just as well. Shrimp, crab and lobster are delicious and low-cal, but any non-oily fish will do, even canned tuna as long as it's packed in water. You can always serve chicken instead of turkey or use everyday iceberg lettuce instead of endive or other exotic greens. I'm not urging you to make these substitutions (I like my diet as is), but I do recognize the economic facts of life that may make them necessary from time to time. Never worry if you end up eating steamed string beans instead of asparagus, or cantaloupe instead of papaya.

Do keep in mind, though, that when you substitute a fish or meat or vegetable for one specified on the diet, the corresponding recipe (if there is one) no longer applies. How, then, should you cook your substitution? Rely on the tried and true diet techniques of broiling, grilling, boiling and steaming foods. And there's nothing wrong with serving vegetables raw.

Liquid. It's important on this or any diet to drink plenty of fluids throughout the day. Six to eight glasses are what I recommend. Liquids help keep food moving along through your system, hydrate cells from the inside so your skin benefits, ease hunger by keeping your stomach partially filled, and give you some of the oral satisfaction you may be missing on a diet.

Plain water from the tap will do, though it's somehow more refreshing and special when it's iced.

As for me, I drink gallons (or so it seems) of weak iced or hot tea to which I add a small amount of artificial sweetener. During the day, when I'm on the go, I usually sip ordinary tea, the kind with caffeine. In the evening I switch to decaffeinated or herbal tea.

Often at lunch, during the afternoon or at cocktail time before dinner—in fact, in almost any situation where the alcohol is flowing—I drink tall glasses of bottled sparkling water, garnished with a strawberry or slice of lemon or lime, or blushed to a pale pretty pink with a splash of sugar-free cranberry juice.

Full-strength fruit juice, however, is not a good alternative for day-long sipping since it is high in calories. Since coffee tends to dehydrate you, it's best to limit yourself to one or two cups a day and not rely on it as a source of fluids. I'd be equally leery about drinking unlimited amounts of dietetic soft drinks; if you're a diet-soda addict, talk to your doctor and be guided by his or her advice.

Though fluids other than coffee or tea with meals are not specified on the menu plans that follow, they are nevertheless extremely important. Tap water, bottled water, weak tea, the choice is yours as long as you drink the required six to eight glasses—but water is really the best.

Vitamin and mineral supplements. I take a multivitamin and mineral preparation, as well as daily calcium supplements. I won't make any recommendations with regard to which vitamins and minerals you should take. However, I feel strongly about calcium. Most women need more of it than they get, especially when they're on a diet. For this reason I've added calcium reminders to the menus. As in all health matters, check with your doctor when in doubt.

One final suggestion. I sometimes suspect that for people like me, weight loss has as much to do with *how* we eat as with *what* we eat. So now that you know something about the contents of my diet, let me tell you a little about my methods.

Most important, I eat slowly. Of course, rushing is sometimes unavoidable, but on hurry-up days when I find it necessary to gulp a protein-drink lunch on the run, I often feel cheated. Not hungry, necessarily, but deprived of an experience that can and should be an enjoyable one, even when I'm dieting. It's so much more satisfying, physically and psychologically, to sit down in a relaxed setting and take my time.

I've discovered that the longer it takes me to eat, the

more it seems I've eaten. To stretch out my meals, I usually spend a few moments admiring the food on my plate before I begin. Then I make a conscious effort to savor each bite. When I dine with others, I try to be the last one finished, never the first. When I'm alone, I prefer to concentrate on the food rather than combine eating with other activities that might interfere with my enjoyment, such as watching television or talking on the phone. I even try to clear my head of plans, projects, problems. Because I've made the most of every bite, I feel satisfied, even if I've eaten small portions.

A FOURTEEN-DAY DIET MEAL PLAN

The menus that follow provide you with two whole weeks of Taylor-style dieting. No two days are alike, though an occasional dish is repeated. Obviously, start with day one and proceed through two, three, four until you've completed the fourteen-day program. Then, if you haven't reached your ideal weight, return to day one.

How many times will you need to repeat the two-week diet in order to reach your goal? I wish I had the answer to that one. It depends on how much weight you need/want to lose, on your metabolism (the rate at which your body burns calories as fuel), and on how physically active you are (the more you exercise, the more calories you'll burn).

Remember, my diet does not promise instant results. Impatience is counterproductive. So is dwelling on all the junk food you love but shouldn't eat—diet or no diet. Rather than focus on how long it will take before you can go off the diet, why not try to make the most of every day that you are on it? Congratulate yourself for every twenty-four hours of success. They'll mount up quickly and you will soon see the wonderful results on the scale, in the fit of your clothes, in the shape of your body, in the state of your mind. I've been through it all, so I know.

Please note that an asterisk next to any dish means that the recipe is included in the recipe section beginning on page 181.

DIET DAY ONE

BREAKFAST

Strawberries, 1 cup sliced
(or 1 cup serving any
fresh fruit other than banana)
Whole-wheat toast, dry, 1 slice
Tea or coffee, splash of skim milk
and artificial sweetener if desired
DON'T FORGET: Calcium supplement

LUNCH

Grilled chicken breast, no skin, 6 ounces
*Artichoke Salad
Tea or coffee, splash of skim milk
and artificial sweetener if desired
OR
*Protein Powder Drink

SNACK

Crudités (your choice of any raw green, yellow
or red vegetables, as much as you can eat) with
*Dip, 2 tablespoons
(select from any of the special dip recipes)

DINNER

*Marinated Grilled Swordfish, 6–8 ounces
*Steamed Vegetables
Brown rice, ½ cup

ANYTIME DURING THE DAY

Skim milk, ½ cup
(use to lighten tea or coffee, or drink as is)

DIET DAY TWO

BREAKFAST

Peach, 1 large sliced (or 1 cup serving
any fresh fruit other than banana)
Whole-wheat toast, dry, 1 slice
Tea or coffee, splash of skim milk
and artificial sweetener if desired
DON'T FORGET: Calcium supplement

LUNCH

Salad of blueberries, ½ cup; cantaloupe,
½ chunked; orange, ½ sliced, with
Low-fat cottage cheese, ½ cup, mixed with
1 tablespoon sour cream
Tea or coffee, splash of skim milk
and artificial sweetener if desired
OR
*Protein Powder Drink

SNACK

Crudités (your choice of any raw green, yellow
or red vegetables, as much as you can eat) with
*Dip, 2 tablespoons
(select from any of the special dip recipes)

DINNER

Grilled lean steak or hamburger, 6–8 ounces,
served on
Whole-wheat toast, 1 slice, spread with
½ tablespoon peanut butter
*Tomato Salad

ANYTIME DURING THE DAY

Skim milk, ½ cup
(use to lighten tea or coffee, or drink as is)

DIET DAY THREE

BREAKFAST

Fresh pineapple, 1 cup chunked (or 1 cup
serving any fresh fruit other than banana)
Whole-wheat toast, dry, 1 slice
Tea or coffee, splash of skim milk
and artificial sweetener if desired
DON'T FORGET: Calcium supplement

LUNCH

Chef's salad of lean roast beef, 1 ounce;
chicken, white meat, 1 ounce;
skim-milk mozzarella cheese, 1 ounce;
tomato, 1 sliced; on lettuce, with
*Dressing, 2 tablespoons
(select from any of the special dressing recipes)
Tea or coffee, splash of skim milk
and artificial sweetener if desired
OR
*Protein Powder Drink

SNACK

Crudités (your choice of any raw green, yellow
or red vegetables, as much as you can eat) with
*Dip, 2 tablespoons
(select from any of the special dip recipes)

DINNER

Grilled shrimp, 6–8 ounces
*Ratatouille
*Minted New Potatoes

ANYTIME DURING THE DAY

Skim milk, ½ cup
(use to lighten tea or coffee, or drink as is)

DIET DAY FOUR

BREAKFAST

Grapefruit, ½ medium (or 1 cup serving
any fresh fruit other than banana)
Whole-wheat toast, dry, 1 slice
Tea or coffee, splash of skim milk
and artificial sweetener if desired
DON'T FORGET: Calcium supplement

LUNCH

Salad of raw spinach, 1½ cups;
hard-cooked eggs, 2; tomato, 1 sliced;
mushrooms, 5–6 sliced; with
*Dressing, 2 tablespoons
(select from any of the special dressing recipes)
Tea or coffee, splash of skim milk
and artificial sweetener if desired
OR
*Protein Powder Drink

SNACK

Crudités (your choice of any raw green, yellow
or red vegetables, as much as you can eat) with
*Dip, 2 tablespoons
(select from any of the special dip recipes)

DINNER

*Spicy Chicken, 6 ounces
Steamed green beans, 1 cup
*Baked Potato Skins

ANYTIME DURING THE DAY

Skim milk, ½ cup
(use to lighten tea or coffee, or drink as is)

DIET DAY FIVE

BREAKFAST

Ripe apricots, 3 medium (or 1 cup serving
any fresh fruit other than banana)
Whole-wheat toast, dry, 1 slice
Tea or coffee, splash of skim milk
and artificial sweetener if desired
DON'T FORGET: Calcium supplement

LUNCH

*Tuna Salad
Tea or coffee, splash of skim milk
and artificial sweetener if desired
OR
*Protein Powder Drink

SNACK

Crudités (your choice of any raw green, yellow
or red vegetables, as much as you can eat) with
*Dip, 2 tablespoons
(select from any of the special dip recipes)

DINNER

Roast turkey breast, 6–8 ounces, with
*Stuffing
*Pureed Summer Squash
Brown rice, ½ cup

ANYTIME DURING THE DAY

Skim milk, ½ cup
(use to lighten tea or coffee, or drink as is)

DIET DAY SIX

BREAKFAST

Cantaloupe, ½ medium (or 1 cup serving
any fresh fruit other than banana)
Whole-wheat toast, dry, 1 slice
Tea or coffee, splash of skim milk
and artificial sweetener if desired
DON'T FORGET: Calcium supplement

LUNCH

Salad of strawberries, 1 cup sliced; apple,
1 medium chunked; orange, 1 small sliced; with
Low-fat cottage cheese, ½ cup, mixed with
1 tablespoon sour cream
Tea or coffee, splash of skim milk
and artificial sweetener if desired
OR
*Protein Powder Drink

SNACK

Crudités (your choice of any raw green, yellow
or red vegetables, as much as you can eat) with
*Dip, 2 tablespoons
(select from any of the special dip recipes)

DINNER

Grilled veal scallops, 6 ounces, seasoned with
lemon juice and fresh herbs
*Spinach Served in Tomato Shell
*Baked Potato Skins

ANYTIME DURING THE DAY

Skim milk, ½ cup
(use to lighten tea or coffee, or drink as is)

DIET DAY SEVEN

BREAKFAST

Strawberries, 1 cup sliced (or 1 cup serving
any fresh fruit other than banana)
Whole-wheat toast, dry, 1 slice
Tea or coffee, splash of skim milk
and artificial sweetener if desired
DON'T FORGET: Calcium supplement

LUNCH

*Curried Chicken Salad
Tea or coffee, splash of skim milk
and artificial sweetener if desired
OR
*Protein Powder Drink

SNACK

Crudités (your choice of any raw green, yellow
or red vegetables, as much as you can eat) with
*Dip, 2 tablespoons
(select from any of the special dip recipes)

DINNER

Grilled fillet of sole, 6–8 ounces
Steamed asparagus, 6–8 spears
*Minted New Potatoes

ANYTIME DURING THE DAY

Skim milk, ½ cup
(use to lighten tea or coffee, or drink as is)

DIET DAY EIGHT

BREAKFAST

Tangerines, 2 small (or 1 cup serving
any fresh fruit other than banana)
Whole-wheat toast, dry, 1 slice
Tea or coffee, splash of skim milk
and artificial sweetener if desired
DON'T FORGET: Calcium supplement

LUNCH

Hamburger, 6 ounces lean, served on
Whole-wheat toast, 1 slice, spread with
½ tablespoon peanut butter
*Tomato Salad
Tea or coffee, splash of skim milk
and artificial sweetener if desired
OR
*Protein Powder Drink

SNACK

Crudités (your choice of any raw green, yellow
or red vegetables, as much as you can eat) with
*Dip, 2 tablespoons
(select from any of the special dip recipes)

DINNER

*Steamed Lobster (or any steamed fish),
6–8 ounces, with
*Liz's Special Mayonnaise, 2 tablespoons
Steamed green beans, 1 cup
Brown rice, ½ cup

ANYTIME DURING THE DAY

Skim milk, ½ cup
(use to lighten tea or coffee, or drink as is)

DIET DAY NINE

BREAKFAST

Kiwi fruit, 2 small (or 1 cup serving
any fresh fruit other than banana)
Whole-wheat toast, dry, 1 slice
Tea or coffee, splash of skim milk
and artificial sweetener if desired
DON'T FORGET: Calcium supplement

LUNCH

Cheese, 2 ounces thinly sliced
(skim-milk mozzarella, cheddar, Swiss, etc.,
mix or match), on
Puffed-wheat crackers, 4
(wrap cheese and cracker in a lettuce leaf
to make a Taylor sandwich!)
Kosher dill pickle, 1; cherry tomatoes, 4–5
Tea or coffee, splash of skim milk
and artificial sweetener if desired
OR
*Protein Powder Drink

SNACK

Crudités (your choice of any raw green, yellow
or red vegetables, as much as you can eat) with
*Dip, 2 tablespoons
(select from any of the special dip recipes)

DINNER

*Red Snapper
*Ratatouille
*Baked Potato Skins

ANYTIME DURING THE DAY

Skim milk, ½ cup
(use to lighten tea or coffee, or drink as is)

DIET DAY TEN

BREAKFAST

Passion fruit, 4 ounces shelled (or 1 cup serving
any fresh fruit other than banana)
Whole-wheat toast, dry, 1 slice
Tea or coffee, splash of skim milk
and artificial sweetener if desired
DON'T FORGET: Calcium supplement

LUNCH

*Cold Crab Salad
Tea or coffee, splash of skim milk
and artificial sweetener if desired
OR
*Protein Powder Drink

SNACK

Crudités (your choice of any raw green, yellow
or red vegetables, as much as you can eat) with
*Dip, 2 tablespoons
(select from any of the special dip recipes)

DINNER

*Grilled Lamb Chops with Raita Sauce
*Pureed Summer Squash
Brown rice, ½ cup

ANYTIME DURING THE DAY

Skim milk, ½ cup
(use to lighten tea or coffee, or drink as is)

DIET DAY ELEVEN

BREAKFAST

Orange, 1 medium (or 1 cup serving
any fresh fruit other than banana)
Whole-wheat toast, dry, 1 slice
Tea or coffee, splash of skim milk
and artificial sweetener if desired
DON'T FORGET: Calcium supplement

LUNCH

Salad of peach, 1 medium sliced; strawberries,
1 cup sliced; apple, 1 medium chunked; with
Low-fat cottage cheese, ½ cup, mixed with
1 tablespoon sour cream
Tea or coffee, splash of skim milk
and artificial sweetener if desired
OR
*Protein Powder Drink

SNACK

Crudités (your choice of any raw green, yellow
or red vegetables, as much as you can eat) with
*Dip, 2 tablespoons
(select from any of the special dip recipes)

DINNER

*Marinated Grilled Swordfish, 6–8 ounces
Steamed broccoli and cauliflower, 1 cup each
*Minted New Potatoes

ANYTIME DURING THE DAY

Skim milk, ½ cup
(use to lighten tea or coffee, or drink as is)

DIET DAY TWELVE

BREAKFAST

Papaya, ½ medium (or 1 cup serving
any fresh fruit other than banana)
Whole-wheat toast, dry, 1 slice
Tea or coffee, splash of skim milk
and artificial sweetener if desired
DON'T FORGET: Calcium supplement

LUNCH

*Tuna Salad
Kosher dill pickle, 1; cherry tomatoes, 4–5
Tea or coffee, splash of skim milk
and artificial sweetener if desired
OR
*Protein Powder Drink

SNACK

Crudités (your choice of any raw green, yellow
or red vegetables, as much as you can eat) with
*Dip, 2 tablespoons
(select from any of the special dip recipes)

DINNER

*Barbecued Squab (½ squab) or chicken,
6 ounces
*Foil-Wrapped Barbecued Vegetables
*Baked Potato Skins

ANYTIME DURING THE DAY

Skim milk, ½ cup
(use to lighten tea or coffee, or drink as is)

DIET DAY THIRTEEN

BREAKFAST

Nectarine, 1 medium (or 1 cup serving
any fresh fruit other than banana)
Whole-wheat toast, dry, 1 slice
Tea or coffee, splash of skim milk
and artificial sweetener if desired
DON'T FORGET: Calcium supplement

LUNCH

Hamburger, 6 ounces lean, served on
Whole-wheat toast, 1 slice, spread with
½ tablespoon peanut butter
*Tomato Salad
Tea or coffee, splash of skim milk
and artificial sweetener if desired
OR
*Protein Powder Drink

SNACK

Crudités (your choice of any raw green, yellow
or red vegetables, as much as you can eat) with
*Dip, 2 tablespoons
(select from any of the special dip recipes)

DINNER

Grilled fillet of sole, 6–8 ounces
*Steamed Snow Peas with Water Chestnuts
Brown rice, ½ cup

ANYTIME DURING THE DAY

Skim milk, ½ cup
(use to lighten tea or coffee, or drink as is)

DIET DAY FOURTEEN

BREAKFAST

Honeydew melon, 2-inch wedge (or 1 cup
serving any fresh fruit other than banana)
Whole-wheat toast, dry, 1 slice
Tea or coffee, splash of skim milk
and artificial sweetener if desired
DON'T FORGET: Calcium supplement

LUNCH

*Curried Egg Salad
Tea or coffee, splash of skim milk
and artificial sweetener if desired
OR
*Protein Powder Drink

SNACK

Crudités (your choice of any raw green, yellow
or red vegetables, as much as you can eat) with
*Dip, 2 tablespoons
(select from any of the special dip recipes)

DINNER

Roast turkey breast, 6–8 ounces, with
*Stuffing
Grilled tomato
*Baked Potato Skins

ANYTIME DURING THE DAY

Skim milk, ½ cup
(use to lighten tea or coffee, or drink as is)

MAINTENANCE

You can imagine how excited I was five years ago when I dropped from 180-odd to 122 pounds. Once I was thin, though, the thrill of success was tempered by uncertainty. Lots of people lose weight, but only a depressingly small percentage keep it off. I couldn't help wondering if I had the discipline to stay in control and never again let an excess pound or two burgeon into a mountain of fat.

So far I haven't had a problem. It seems that after months of eating moderately, many of my old unhealthy attitudes toward food vanished. Eating more nutritiously and more moderately had become second nature.

To paraphrase all the doctors I've consulted and all the diet books I've read, a diet can win the battle, but the war isn't over until you reeducate your appetite. Apparently, all those months of eating smaller portions of low-fat food did just that: reeducated my appetite.

Oh, I still adore chocolate, and fried chicken with mashed potatoes, but I don't crave them and I certainly don't *live* on them. Why should I, now that I've developed a taste for other foods that are healthier?

As you will see when you turn to the suggested maintenance menus, the food I eat today isn't all that different in type or amount from what I ate when I was dieting. The major difference in maintenance breakfasts is that they often include cereal or a bran muffin, and cream cheese or a dab of butter. Maintenance lunches are about the same as diet lunches. And maintenance dinners are similar to the ones I lost weight on, except that the meat portions are somewhat larger and there is almost always a terrific—but low-cal—dessert.

The menus that follow should get you off to a good start. After that, improvise your own maintenance plan, using my menus as guidelines. Be sure to include moderate-sized portions of a wide variety of different foods, with the emphasis on broiled or grilled poultry and seafood, steamed or raw vegetables, and lots of fruit. Have starchy vegetables and pasta, but don't overdo it. Breads and cereals should be whole-grain. If you find yourself gaining weight on your personal maintenance plan, eat smaller portions of everything rather than eliminate any one food group. (High-calorie desserts are the exception; those you can always do without.)

You won't believe it until you've actually started, but maintenance eating is not a hardship.

After weeks or months of dieting, your body will have accommodated itself—as mine did—to a different, lighter way of eating: one that makes you feel more energetic, and better able to deal with all the challenges and joys life throws your way.

Again, please note that an asterisk next to any dish means that the recipe is included in the recipe section beginning on page 181.

MAINTENANCE DAY ONE

BREAKFAST

Unsweetened dry cereal, 1 ounce
(or my favorite mix of ½ ounce Special K
and ½ ounce All-Bran)
Grapefruit, ½ medium, *or* ¼ cup orange juice
Tea or coffee, splash of skim milk
and artificial sweetener if desired
DON'T FORGET: Calcium supplement

LUNCH

Cheese, 2 ounces thinly sliced
(skim-milk mozzarella, cheddar, Swiss, etc.,
mix or match), on
Puffed-wheat crackers, 4
(wrap cheese and cracker in a lettuce leaf
to make a Taylor sandwich!)
Kosher dill pickle, 1; cherry tomatoes, 4–5
Tea or coffee, splash of skim milk
and artificial sweetener if desired
OR
*Protein Powder Drink

SNACK

Crudités (your choice of any raw green, yellow
or red vegetables, as much as you can eat) with
*Dip, 2 tablespoons
(select from any of the special dip recipes)

DINNER

*Lamb Chops with Raita Sauce
Spinach/mushroom salad with your choice of
*Dressing, 2 tablespoons
(select from any of the special dressing recipes)
Baked potato with 1 tablespoon sour cream
*Baked Peach with Raspberry Sauce

ANYTIME DURING THE DAY

Skim milk, ½ cup (use on cereal,
to lighten tea or coffee, or drink as is)

MAINTENANCE DAY TWO

BREAKFAST

Bran muffin, 1 medium, spread with
2 teaspoons low-cal cream cheese
Grapefruit, ½ medium, *or* ¼ cup orange juice
Tea or coffee, splash of skim milk
and artificial sweetener if desired
DON'T FORGET: Calcium supplement

LUNCH

Broiled or grilled jumbo shrimp, 6, with
*Liz's Special Mayonnaise
Puffed-wheat crackers, 3–4
Tea or coffee, splash of skim milk
and artificial sweetener if desired
OR
*Protein Powder Drink

SNACK

Crudités (your choice of any raw green, yellow
or red vegetables, as much as you can eat) with
*Dip, 2 tablespoons
(select from any of the special dip recipes)

DINNER

Pasta, 1½ cups with
*Tomato Sauce
Mixed green salad with
*Roquefort Dressing, 2 tablespoons
*Apple Tart

ANYTIME DURING THE DAY

Skim milk, ½ cup
(use to lighten tea or coffee, or drink as is)

MAINTENANCE DAY THREE

BREAKFAST

Peach, 1 large (or 1 cup serving
any fresh fruit other than banana)
Whole-wheat toast, 1 slice,
with 1 teaspoon butter
Tea or coffee, splash of skim milk
and artificial sweetener if desired
DON'T FORGET: Calcium supplement

LUNCH

Chef's salad of lean roast beef, 1 ounce; chicken,
white meat, 1 ounce; skim-milk mozzarella,
1 ounce; tomato, 1 sliced; on lettuce, with
*Horseradish Dressing, 2 tablespoons
Whole-wheat toast, dry, 1 slice
Tea or coffee, splash of skim milk
and artificial sweetener if desired
OR
*Protein Powder Drink

SNACK

Crudités (your choice of any raw green, yellow
or red vegetables, as much as you can eat) with
*Dip, 2 tablespoons
(select from any of the special dip recipes)

DINNER

Grilled salmon, 6–8 ounces
Steamed broccoli and cauliflower, 1 cup each
*Baked Potato Skins
*Orange Soufflé

ANYTIME DURING THE DAY

Skim milk, ½ cup
(use to lighten tea or coffee, or drink as is)

MAINTENANCE DAY FOUR

BREAKFAST

Unsweetened dry cereal, 1 ounce
(or my favorite mix of ½ ounce Special K
and ½ ounce All-Bran)
Grapefruit, ½ medium, *or* ¼ cup orange juice
Tea or coffee, splash of skim milk
and artificial sweetener if desired
DON'T FORGET: Calcium supplement

LUNCH

Scrambled eggs, 2, with
Very crisp bacon, 3 slices, on
Well-toasted English muffin
Grilled tomato, 1 medium
Tea or coffee, splash of skim milk
and artificial sweetener if desired
OR
*Protein Powder Drink

SNACK

Crudités (your choice of any raw green, yellow
or red vegetables, as much as you can eat) with
*Dip, 2 tablespoons
(select from any of the special dip recipes)

DINNER

*Red Snapper
Corn, 1 small ear
Salad of mixed greens, 1½ cups, with
*Dressing, 2 tablespoons
(select from any of the special dressing recipes)
Seedless red grapes, ½ cup

ANYTIME DURING THE DAY

Skim milk, ½ cup (use on cereal,
to lighten tea or coffee, or drink as is)

MAINTENANCE DAY FIVE

BREAKFAST

Raspberries, 1 cup (or 1 cup serving
any fresh fruit other than banana)
Whole-wheat toast, 1 slice,
with 1 teaspoon butter
Tea or coffee, splash of skim milk
and artificial sweetener if desired
DON'T FORGET: Calcium supplement

LUNCH

Grilled lean hamburger, 6 ounces, served on
Whole-wheat toast, 1 slice, spread with
½ tablespoon peanut butter
*Tomato Salad
Tea or coffee, splash of skim milk
and artificial sweetener if desired
OR
*Protein Powder Drink

SNACK

Crudités (your choice of any raw green, yellow
or red vegetables, as much as you can eat) with
*Dip, 2 tablespoons
(select from any of the special dip recipes)

DINNER

*Poached Garlic Chicken
*Pureed Summer Squash
Brown rice, ½ cup
Tofu "ice cream," ½ cup, with *Raspberry Sauce

ANYTIME DURING THE DAY

Skim milk, ½ cup
(use to lighten tea or coffee, or drink as is)

MAINTENANCE DAY SIX

BREAKFAST

Bran muffin, 1 medium, spread with
2 teaspoons low-cal cream cheese
Grapefruit, ½ medium, *or* ¼ cup orange juice
Tea or coffee, splash of skim milk
and artificial sweetener if desired
DON'T FORGET: Calcium supplement

LUNCH

Fruit salad made with orange, 1 medium sliced;
cantaloupe, ½ chunked; apple, 1 medium
chunked; berries, handful, with
Low-fat cottage cheese, 1 cup, mixed with
1 tablespoon sour cream
Tea or coffee, splash of skim milk
and artificial sweetener if desired
OR
*Protein Powder Drink

SNACK

Crudités (your choice of any raw green, yellow
or red vegetables, as much as you can eat) with
*Dip, 2 tablespoons
(select from any of the special dip recipes)

DINNER

*Steamed Lobster, 6 ounces
*Steamed Cucumber with Dill
*Minted New Potatoes
*Chocolate Fantasy

ANYTIME DURING THE DAY

Skim milk, ½ cup
(use to lighten tea or coffee, or drink as is)

MAINTENANCE DAY SEVEN

BREAKFAST

Unsweetened dry cereal, 1 ounce
(or, my favorite mix of ½ ounce Special K
and ½ ounce All-Bran)
Grapefruit, ½ medium, *or* ¼ cup orange juice
Tea or coffee, splash of skim milk
and artificial sweetener if desired
DON'T FORGET: Calcium supplement

LUNCH

*Curried Chicken Salad
Puffed-wheat crackers, 3–4
Tea or coffee, splash of skim milk
and artificial sweetener if desired
OR
*Protein Powder Drink

SNACK

Crudités (your choice of any raw green, yellow
or red vegetables, as much as you can eat) with
*Dip, 2 tablespoons
(select from any of the special dip recipes)

DINNER

Grilled veal scallops, 6 ounces, seasoned with
lemon juice and fresh herbs
*Ratatouille
*Baked Potato Skins
*Baked Apple

ANYTIME DURING THE DAY

Skim milk, ½ cup (use on cereal,
to lighten tea or coffee, or drink as is)

Entrées

POACHED GARLIC CHICKEN

4 SERVINGS

4-pound chicken, cut into 8 pieces
¼ stick low-cal margarine
5 large unpeeled garlic cloves, crushed
5 tablespoons balsamic or other vinegar
1 cup dry white wine
2 teaspoons mustard
1 heaping teaspoon tomato paste
1 teaspoon arrowroot
2 teaspoons water
¼ pint low-cal sour cream
Salt substitute or salt, and pepper
2 tomatoes, peeled and seeded

Brown chicken in hot melted margarine. Add garlic, cover pan, and cook over low heat for 20 minutes or until chicken is tender. Remove chicken to serving dish and keep warm. Pour all but a tablespoon of margarine from pan and add vinegar, stirring and scraping up any brown bits from bottom. Turn up heat and boil until liquid is reduced to about 2 tablespoons. Add wine, mustard and tomato paste, mix well, and continue to boil. Mix arrowroot with 2 teaspoons water, combine with sour cream in a small pan, and simmer gently until thickened. Remove from heat and pour vinegar mixture through sieve into small pan. With a whisk, mix vinegar and sour cream mixtures together and add salt and pepper to taste. Cut tomatoes into long thin strips and add to sauce. If necessary, warm sauce before spooning over chicken.

SPICY CHICKEN

4 SERVINGS

2 teaspoons curry powder
1 teaspoon cumin
½ teaspoon ground ginger
½ teaspoon turmeric
½ clove garlic, crushed
1 onion, chopped
1 teaspoon fresh ginger, grated
1 medium chicken, cut into serving pieces and skinned

Combine dry ingredients with garlic, onion and fresh grated ginger. Coat chicken with mixture and refrigerate for 2 hours, preferably longer. Place on moderately hot barbecue grill or broil in oven approximately 30 minutes or until done, turning once.

CURRIED CHICKEN SALAD

1 SERVING

6-ounce chicken breast, broiled or stewed, skin removed
½ crisp green apple, chunked
2 ribs celery, chopped
2 tablespoons curried Liz's Special Mayonnaise (#1 or #2) or commercial low-cal mayonnaise
Ripe mango (optional)

Slice chicken breast into thin strips. Toss with apple, celery and mayonnaise. Garnish with sliced ripe mango if desired.

CRAB SALAD

1 LARGE OR 2 SMALL SERVINGS

2-pound live crab or 2-pound cooked crab, intact
Juice of 1 small lemon
2 teaspoons balsamic vinegar
1/2 teaspoon mustard
Fresh breadcrumbs, made from 1 slice whole-wheat
  bread
Salt substitute or salt, and pepper
Few sprigs fresh parsley, chopped
Several leaves iceberg lettuce
3–4 cherry tomatoes (optional)
Lemon wedges (optional)

Place live crab in saucepan with enough water to cover, and boil for 30 minutes. Remove and refrigerate until cool enough to handle. Then, with crab on its back, twist off legs and claws. Crack around edge, and remove belly shell and small sac near head of crab and discard. Scoop meat from bottom shell, placing light meat in one bowl and dark meat in another. Wash and dry top shell. Crack large claws but do not remove meat. Reserve cracked claws for garnish, if desired. With a skewer, ice pick or other long, sharp tool, pull meat from legs and place in bowl with white meat.

For the dressing: Combine brown meat with lemon juice, vinegar, mustard and enough breadcrumbs to hold mixture together. Add salt and pepper to taste. Combine with white meat and parsley and toss lightly.

To assemble: Line top shell with iceberg lettuce. Mound dressing into shell. Garnish with cracked claws, cherry tomatoes and lemon wedges if desired. Serve with Liz's Special Mayonnaise or commercial low-cal mayonnaise.

CURRIED EGG SALAD

1 LARGE SERVING

1 small bunch watercress
1 Belgian endive, chopped
½ teaspoon ground sesame seeds
2 hard-boiled eggs
2 tablespoons curried Liz's Special Mayonnaise (#1
   or #2) or commercial low-cal mayonnaise
Paprika

Toss watercress, endive and sesame seeds together and arrange on plate. Slice eggs into quarters and place in pinwheel shape on greens. Top with mayonnaise. Dust with paprika.

GRILLED LAMB CHOPS WITH RAITA SAUCE

1 SERVING

3 very small, very lean lamb chops
¼ cup plain low-fat yogurt
2 inches cucumber, peeled and finely diced
2 sprigs fresh mint, finely chopped
½ clove garlic, crushed
Salt substitute or salt, and pepper to taste

Grill or broil lamb chops on a *hot* barbecue or grill to medium rare, approximately 2–5 minutes on each side. As chops cook, combine all other ingredients to make the sauce. Serve as an accompaniment to the lamb.

MARINATED GRILLED SWORDFISH

1 SERVING

Juice and zest of ½ lemon or lime
½ teaspoon fresh dill, finely chopped
¼ teaspoon freshly ground black pepper
6- to 8-ounce swordfish steak
Lemon or lime (optional)
Parsley (optional)

Combine lemon or lime juice and zest, dill and pepper. Pour over swordfish and marinate for 30 minutes. Place on hot barbecue grill or under broiler and cook until flaky, about 4 minutes each side. Serve as is or with Asparagus Sauce. Garnish with lemon or lime slices and parsley if desired.

STEAMED LOBSTER

1 SERVING

1½ pound lobster (to yield approximately 6 ounces
meat) or 6 ounces canned or frozen lobster

In a saucepan large enough to accommodate lobster,
bring 3 inches water to a boil. Add lobster, cover pan,
turn down heat, and simmer for 15 minutes. Remove
from heat and immerse in cold water. Serve with 2
tablespoons Watercress Sauce or other special sauce.

RED SNAPPER

1 SERVING

1 medium leek, finely chopped
2 ounces morel mushrooms, finely chopped (or
  use regular mushrooms)
½ teaspoon fresh chervil, finely chopped
2 tablespoons dry white wine
Salt substitute or salt, and pepper to taste
6 ounces red snapper, filleted
Chopped parsley (optional)
Lemon wedges (optional)

Combine leek, mushrooms, chervil, wine, salt and pepper and stuff into fish. Wrap loosely in foil. Place on
barbecue grill and cook for 10 minutes, or in moderate
oven and cook for 15 minutes or until fish is flaky.
Unwrap, remove skin from fish, garnish with parsley
and lemon wedges, and serve as is or with Red Snapper
Sauce.

RED SNAPPER SAUCE

1 SERVING

Juice from foil-cooked fish
¼ cup fish stock or bottled clam juice
1 tablespoon crème fraîche or sour cream
1 teaspoon arrowroot mixed with 1 tablespoon
    water

Pour juice from cooked fish into small saucepan; add
fish stock or clam juice and boil until reduced by half.
Remove from heat and add crème fraîche or sour cream
and arrowroot-water mixture. Stir over gentle heat (do
not boil) until sauce begins to thicken. Pour over fish
and serve. The fish dish looks more attractive if garnished with lemon wedges and watercress.

BARBECUED SQUAB

6 SERVINGS

Juice and zest of 1 lemon
3 medium cloves garlic, crushed
1 tablespoon low-sodium soy sauce
2 teaspoons fresh horseradish, grated
2 teaspoons Worcestershire sauce
1 teaspoon paprika
3 squab, cut in half
Lemon wedges (optional)
Fresh rosemary (optional)

Combine first six ingredients. Marinate squab in mixture for at least 2 hours, preferably longer. Place squab on hot barbecue grill or broil for about 20 minutes, turning once. Serve immediately, garnished with lemon wedges and fresh rosemary if desired.

This recipe can also be made with chicken. Use approximately 1½ pounds breasts, legs, thighs.

You've come a long way, baby, on the inside...but
there's a lot of work to be done on the outside—my
first photo after the Betty Ford Center.
(David McGough/DMI)

Trying to hide my size behind a rose. Who was I kidding?
Did I think that was a waist I was belting in?
(Left: Ron Galella/Ron Galella, Ltd.;
right: Alan Berliner/ABSI)

Caught by the unforgiving camera once again.
(Ron Galella/Ron Galella, Ltd.)

Greeting "Mighty Mo," Maureen Stapleton, a great actress
and a dear friend. Note my hairdo (or rather lack of one),
which is so indicative of a loss of self-esteem.
(Photograph by Raimondo Borea)

Another special friend and colleague, Carol Burnett.
I'm in one of my cover-ups—that didn't....
(John Paschal/DMI)

My first public appearance after
the Betty Ford Center. With Betty,
Gregory Peck, Martha Graham,
and Polly Bergen—
you would think I was pregnant!
(© 1987 *Joan Tedeschi*)

Attending a party with my old friend Roddy McDowall.
(Kevin Winter/DMI)

My dear friend Rock—taken by my son Christopher on
the set of *The Mirror Crack'd*.

Special moments with my mother at Lincoln
Center. The height of my self-esteem and
self-image, which brought an inner happiness.
(Both photos David McGough/DMI)

Burt Reynolds and I at a charity benefit in Beverly Hills.
(© *Chris Hunter*)

George and I at my fifty-fifth birthday party, given by my good friends
Carole and Burt Bacharach (*top*); Christopher, my son, and I share many
wonderful moments...including the same birthday (*bottom*).
(*Both photos* © 1987 *Michael Jacobs/MJP*)

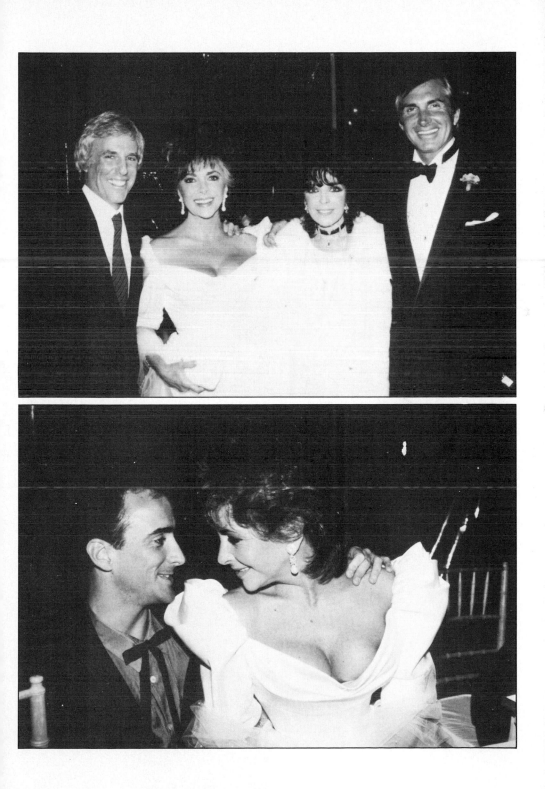

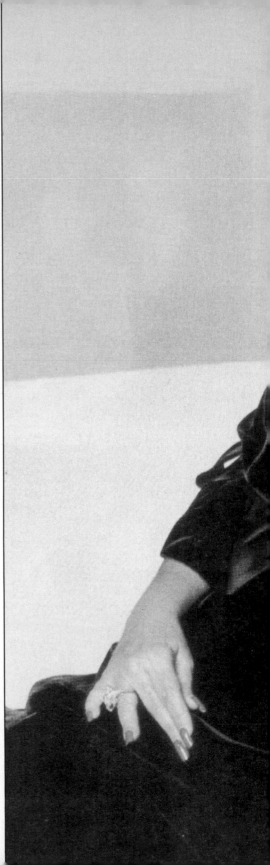

"To thine own self be true."
(© 1985 Terry O'Neill/
Woodfin Camp & Associates)

One of the major high points of my life—after living
through the devastating changes and discovering the "click,"
my entire life has turned around completely.
A very special happening: the announcement of my perfume,
Elizabeth Taylor's Passion, on January 14, 1987, in New York.
(Linda Solomon)

TUNA SALAD

1 SERVING

3½ ounce can water-packed tuna
1 teaspoon tomato paste
1½ tablespoons Liz's Special Mayonnaise or commercial low-cal mayonnaise
2 scallions, chopped
2 ribs celery, diced
½ medium pink grapefruit
3–4 leaves lettuce
2 scallions, whole

Drain tuna and mash with a fork. Add tomato paste to mayonnaise, stir until well blended and combine, along with chopped scallions and celery, with tuna. Carefully remove grapefruit segments, discard whitish pith, and add to tuna mixture. Reserve grapefruit shell.

To assemble: Arrange lettuce leaves on plate, pile tuna mixture into grapefruit shell, and place shell on lettuce. Slice green ends of whole scallions into "fringes" and arrange in fan shape as garnish for salad.

STUFFING FOR TURKEY OR CHICKEN

2 SERVINGS

½ cup celery, finely chopped
½ cup carrots, coarsely chopped
½ cup mushrooms, sliced
½ cup onion, chopped
1 large clove garlic, crushed
½ cup chicken broth or bouillon
2 slices whole-wheat bread, crumbed (use blender)
2 egg whites
½ cup water chestnuts
1 teaspoon fresh parsley, chopped
½ teaspoon rosemary
½ teaspoon thyme
Salt substitute or salt, and pepper to taste

Steam all vegetables but water chestnuts in chicken broth until tender (3–5 minutes). Allow to cool. Mix in breadcrumbs, egg whites, water chestnuts, herbs and salt and pepper. Bake in 350° oven for 40 minutes or until brown and crunchy. Serve with barbecued or roast turkey or chicken.

PROTEIN POWDER DRINK

1 SERVING

2 tablespoons protein powder (available in many
  large supermarkets and all health-food stores)
2 teaspoons malted milk
2 teaspoons carob powder
1 packet sugar substitute
2 drops vanilla
4 ounces water
Ice cubes

Combine dry ingredients and vanilla with water. Whir in blender at high speed until well mixed. Add ice cubes, one at a time, until mixture becomes thick and creamy.

Vegetables

ARTICHOKE SALAD

1 LARGE SERVING

$\frac{1}{2}$ cup frozen or canned, drained artichoke hearts
$\frac{1}{2}$ cup tomato, cut into bite-size chunks
$\frac{1}{2}$ cup onion, coarsely chopped
$\frac{1}{2}$ teaspoon fresh sage, finely chopped
Salt substitute or salt, and pepper

Arrange artichoke hearts and tomato on plate. Sprinkle with onion, then sage. Season with salt and pepper to taste. Spoon Low-Cal Vinaigrette or Oil-Free Vinaigrette over salad and serve.

FOIL-WRAPPED BARBECUED VEGETABLES

1 SERVING

$\frac{1}{4}$ pound mushrooms, sliced
$\frac{1}{4}$ pound celeriac, cut into bite-size pieces
1 medium onion, coarsely chopped
1 teaspoon fresh thyme, finely chopped
1 teaspoon low-sodium soy sauce

Combine ingredients and place on sheet of aluminum foil; fold foil to seal. Cook on barbecue grill or in moderate oven for 10–15 minutes. Don't overcook; vegetables are best when still slightly crunchy.

STEAMED CUCUMBER WITH DILL

1 SERVING

1 medium cucumber
2 teaspoons fresh dill, finely chopped
Pinch salt substitute or salt
Sprinkle lemon pepper

Peel and slice cucumber into 1-inch rounds. Sprinkle with dill, salt and lemon pepper. Steam until just slightly crisp.

BAKED POTATO SKINS

1 SERVING

2 medium potatoes
1 tablespoon grated Parmesan cheese
Salt substitute or salt, and pepper

Bake potatoes in 400° oven or microwave until cooked. Slice each in half lengthwise while still hot. With a spoon, scoop out most of the potato, leaving just a thin layer adhering to skin. Sprinkle skins with cheese and season to taste with salt and pepper. Place on barbecue grill or under broiler until brown and crunchy. For best flavor and texture, serve immediately.

STEAMED SNOW PEAS WITH WATER CHESTNUTS

1 LARGE OR 2 SMALL SERVINGS

1/2 pound prepared snow peas
2 water chestnuts, sliced
2 teaspoons low-sodium soy sauce

Steam snow peas 3–4 minutes or until slightly tender. Remove from heat and toss with water chestnuts and soy sauce in a warm bowl.

SPINACH SERVED IN TOMATO SHELL

1 SERVING

1 medium beefsteak tomato
Fresh or frozen chopped spinach to equal 1 cup
    when cooked
1/2 tablespoon fresh pine nuts
1/4 teaspoon nutmeg
Salt substitute or salt

Slice blossom end from tomato. Scoop out pulp and seeds and discard. Steam or simmer spinach until tender, and drain. Mix in pine nuts, nutmeg and salt to taste. Spoon into tomato shell and bake in moderate oven for 10 minutes.

MINTED NEW POTATOES

1 SERVING

4 small new potatoes, scrubbed
1 large sprig fresh mint
Chopped chives
Salt substitute or salt

Place potatoes in saucepan with enough water to cover. Crush mint leaves and add to water. Simmer for 15 minutes or until potatoes are cooked. Drain potatoes and serve hot, sprinkled with chopped chives and salt to taste.

RATATOUILLE

4 SERVINGS

1½ cups eggplant, cut into 1-inch cubes
1½ cups green beans, coarsely chopped
1½ cups onions, coarsely chopped
1½ cups mushrooms, quartered
1 tablespoon tomato paste
1 teaspoon fresh coriander, chopped
Salt substitute or salt, and pepper

Place water ½ inch deep in saucepan, add first five ingredients and simmer until soft. (Add a bit more water if necessary.) Stir in coriander and add salt and pepper to taste. Serve hot. Refrigerate leftovers; they're great hot or cold!

PUREED SUMMER SQUASH

1 SERVING

2 medium summer squash
Salt substitute or salt, and pepper

Steam squash until tender. Remove to a bowl and mash with a fork until smooth. Add salt and pepper to taste.

TOMATO SALAD

1 SERVING

1 medium beefsteak tomato
1 small onion
Fresh basil, finely chopped
Lemon pepper

Slice tomato and onion into thin rounds. Arrange on plate, alternating tomato and onion rounds in overlapping circles. Sprinkle with basil and add lemon pepper, both to taste.

STEAMED VEGETABLES

1 LARGE SERVING

½ cup zucchini or summer squash, cut into bite-
　size pieces
½ cup broccoli, cut into bite-size pieces
½ cup cauliflowerets, cut into bite-size pieces
Lemon juice
Freshly ground black pepper
1 tablespoon low-sodium soy sauce (optional)

Steam vegetables 2–4 minutes. (Do not overcook; they're best when still slightly crisp.) Remove from steamer and add lemon juice and pepper to taste. Drizzle with soy sauce, if desired, and toss to mix. Or try with one of the special dressing recipes.

Dips, Sauces, Dressings

ASPARAGUS SAUCE

½ pound fresh asparagus
¼ cup chicken stock or bouillon
1 teaspoon low-fat sour cream
Salt substitute or salt, and pepper

Snap off and discard tough ends of asparagus. Slice remainder into 1-inch lengths and simmer in chicken stock or bouillon until tender. Allow to cool slightly, then place in blender, add sour cream and whir until pureed. Add salt and pepper to taste. Warm over low heat and serve as sauce for fish or chicken.

TANGY BLUE-CHEESE DIP OR DRESSING

8 ounces blue cheese, crumbled
4 teaspoons low-cal sour cream
2 teaspoons vinegar
1 shallot, minced
Salt substitute or salt, and pepper

Combine first four ingredients in blender and whir until smooth and creamy. Season to taste with salt and pepper. Chill and use as a dip for crudités, or as dressing for vegetables or salad.

GARLIC CREAM DIP OR DRESSING

8 ounces low-cal cream cheese, crumbled
2 tablespoons plain low-fat yogurt
2 tablespoons fresh chives, chopped
¼ cup skim milk
1 clove garlic, crushed
Salt substitute or salt, and pepper to taste

Place all ingredients in a blender and whir until smooth and creamy. Chill and use as a dip for crudités or as dressing for vegetables or salad.

HORSERADISH DRESSING

½ cup Liz's Special Mayonnaise or commercial low-
   cal mayonnaise
1 teaspoon fresh horseradish, finely grated
½ teaspoon prepared mustard
2 drops hot sauce

Combine ingredients and mix well. Serve warm on vegetables or chilled on salad.

MOCK CAVIAR DIP OR DRESSING

1 small jar lumpfish roe (real caviar is too oily)
1 cup plain low-fat yogurt
Lemon juice
Salt substitute or salt, and pepper

Stir lumpfish roe into yogurt. Add lemon juice, salt and pepper to taste. Chill and use as a dip for crudités, or warm and spoon over plain steamed vegetables.

CREAM CHEESE AND CHIVES DIP OR DRESSING

8 ounces low-cal cream cheese, crumbled
1 tablespoon low-cal sour cream
2 tablespoons fresh chives, chopped
Skim milk
Salt substitute or salt, and pepper

Combine cream cheese, sour cream and chives in blender, and whir. Add enough skim milk to bring to "dip" consistency and whir again until creamy. Add salt and pepper to taste. Chill and serve as a dip for crudités or as dressing for vegetables or salad.

LIZ'S SPECIAL MAYONNAISE

1 whole egg
1 egg yolk
1 tablespoon balsamic or other vinegar
Juice of 1 lemon
2 cloves garlic, peeled and crushed
½ teaspoon dry mustard
½ teaspoon Worcestershire sauce
1 cup safflower oil
Salt substitute or salt, and pepper
Artificial sweetener
½ cup skim milk

Place egg and egg yolk, vinegar, lemon juice, garlic, mustard and Worcestershire sauce in blender and whir till well mixed. With blender on high speed, add oil a little at a time. (Mixture will be very thick.) Remove to a bowl and add salt, pepper and artificial sweetener to taste. Pour in skim milk and stir to mix thoroughly. Store in airtight container in refrigerator until needed; will keep well for up to 6 weeks.

CURRIED MAYONNAISE #1

1 cup Liz's Special Mayonnaise or commercial low-
 cal mayonnaise
2 tablespoons safflower oil
2 tablespoons vinegar
1 small onion, finely chopped
2 teaspoons curry powder
2 teaspoons lemon juice
Salt substitute or salt, and pepper

Combine first six ingredients and stir until well blended. Add salt and pepper to taste. Chill and use as a dip with crudités or as dressing for vegetables or salad. Can also be used in Curried Chicken Salad and Curried Egg Salad.

CURRIED MAYONNAISE #2

1 cup Liz's Special Mayonnaise or commercial low-
 cal mayonnaise
2 teaspoons curry powder
1 teaspoon low-cal apricot preserves
Juice of ½ lime or lemon

Combine ingredients. Stir to mix thoroughly. Use to make Curried Chicken Salad or Curried Egg Salad or as a dip.

TARTARE DIP OR DRESSING

1 cup Liz's Special Mayonnaise or commercial low-
   cal mayonnaise
½ small onion, finely chopped
2 tablespoons gherkins, finely chopped
2 tablespoons capers, finely chopped
1 tablespoon fresh parsley, finely chopped
Lemon juice
Salt substitute or salt, and pepper

Combine first five ingredients and stir well to blend.
Add lemon juice, salt and pepper to taste. Chill and use
as a dip for crudités or dressing for salad.

TOMATO DIP OR DRESSING

8 ounces "lite" or dietetic tomato catsup
3 tablespoons low-cal sour cream
½ small onion, chopped
1 teaspoon Dijon mustard
1 clove garlic, crushed
2 tablespoons fresh parsley, chopped

Combine ingredients and whir in blender until pureed. Chill and serve as a dip for crudités or as dressing for vegetables or salad. Or warm and spoon over steak.

ROQUEFORT DIP OR DRESSING

1 cup plain low-fat yogurt
2 ounces Roquefort or blue cheese, crumbled
2 tablespoons balsamic or other vinegar
1 large clove garlic, crushed
1 teaspoon Worcestershire sauce
$\frac{1}{2}$ teaspoon dry mustard
Artificial sweetener
Freshly ground black pepper

Place all ingredients but sweetener and pepper in blender and whir until smooth. Add sweetener and pepper to taste. Use as a dip for crudités or as dressing for vegetables or salad.

MUSTARD DIP OR DRESSING

1 cup Liz's Special Mayonnaise or commercial low-
   cal mayonnaise
2 tablespoons low-cal sour cream
2 tablespoons French Moutarde de Meaux or other
   seeded mustard

Stir all ingredients together until well blended. Chill and use as a dip for crudités or as dressing for vegetables or salad.

TOMATO SAUCE

2 large, fresh plum tomatoes, peeled
2 ribs celery, chopped
1 carrot, chopped
1 small onion, chopped
1 clove garlic
Juice of ½ lemon
1 teaspoon Worcestershire sauce
1 bay leaf
1 teaspoon fresh basil, chopped
Few sprigs fresh parsley, chopped
1 packet artificial sweetener

Place all ingredients in heavy-bottomed pan and simmer for 30 minutes. If mixture is too thin, reduce by further cooking. Serve over pasta or over chicken, fish or steak.

LOW-CAL VINAIGRETTE

5 tablespoons chicken stock or bouillon
1 tablespoon vegetable oil
1 tablespoon lemon juice
1 tablespoon balsamic or other vinegar
1 large clove garlic, crushed
$\frac{1}{2}$ tablespoon chives
$\frac{1}{2}$ teaspoon chervil
Dash Tabasco sauce
Salt substitute or salt, and pepper

Combine first seven ingredients and set aside to marinate at least 2 hours. Add Tabasco, salt and pepper to taste. Stir briskly to mix before serving.

OIL-FREE VINAIGRETTE

½ cup balsamic or tarragon vinegar
½ peeled cucumber, coarsely chopped
1 green onion, coarsely chopped
2 cloves garlic, crushed
1 teaspoon Worcestershire sauce
½ teaspoon fresh parsley, chopped
½ teaspoon fresh basil, chopped
Artificial sweetener
Salt substitute or salt, and pepper

Place first seven ingredients in blender and whir until smooth. Add artificial sweetener, salt and pepper to taste.

Note: For a creamier vinaigrette, add two egg whites to other ingredients before blending.

WATERCRESS SAUCE OR DIP

¼ cup Liz's Special Mayonnaise or commercial low-
   cal mayonnaise
1 tablespoon watercress, finely chopped

Combine ingredients. Stir to mix thoroughly. Use as a dip for crudités or serve with lobster.

Desserts

BAKED APPLE

1 SERVING

1 medium Granny Smith apple
1 tablespoon currants or raisins
Zest of ½ orange, chopped
1 packet artificial sweetener
½ teaspoon cinnamon

Wash and core apple. With a sharp knife, score skin horizontally around fattest part of apple to prevent it from bursting during cooking. Mix other ingredients and pack into apple. Place apple in ovenproof baking dish filled with ½ inch water. Bake in 200° oven approximately 1 hour, or until soft.

APPLE TART

4 SERVINGS

For the pastry:
1 scant cup whole-meal flour
1 scant cup plain flour
½ cup low-cal margarine
Pinch salt substitute or salt
2 egg whites
Water

For the filling:
2 large green apples
2 apricots
1 teaspoon raisins
½ teaspoon cinnamon
½ teaspoon allspice
½ teaspoon ground cloves
½ packet artificial sweetener
3 tablespoons low-cal apricot preserves (for glaze)

Combine flours, margarine and salt, and mix in food processor to consistency of fine breadcrumbs. Add egg whites and water to make a firm dough. (Dough should not be too moist; though drier dough is more difficult to work with, it produces flakier, more tender pastry.) Chill in refrigerator for at least 30 minutes.

In the meantime peel, quarter, core and thinly slice apples. Halve apricots, remove pits from them and slice them.

Roll out pastry, fit into an 8-inch tart plate. Trim away excess with a knife. Bake for 10 minutes at 190°. Remove from oven and place raisins, apple and apricot slices in pastry, arranging top layers in neatly overlapping circles. Dust with cinnamon, allspice, cloves, artificial sweetener. Return to oven for 20 minutes, brush top with apricot preserves and bake another 5 minutes. Allow to cool before serving.

BAKED PEACH WITH RASPBERRY SAUCE

1 SERVING

1 large firm peach
2 tablespoons water
Sprinkle artificial sweetener
Pinch allspice
½ teaspoon lemon zest, grated
Fresh mint leaves (optional)
Fresh raspberries (optional)

Slice peach in half lengthwise and remove pit. Place halves in ovenproof baking dish with water, artificial sweetener, allspice and lemon zest. Cover dish with aluminum foil and bake in 300° oven for 20–25 minutes or until soft. Serve with Raspberry Sauce. Garnish with mint leaves and whole raspberries if desired.

RASPBERRY SAUCE

1 cup fresh raspberries
Juice of ½ lemon
2 packets artificial sweetener

Whir all ingredients in blender until smooth. Pour onto plate. Drain baked peach halves, slice and arrange on plate.

ORANGE SOUFFLÉ

4 SERVINGS

4 oranges
3 tablespoons low-cal margarine
5 tablespoons flour
Zest of 1 orange, grated
2 packets artificial sweetener
2 egg whites

Slice approximately 1 inch off tops of oranges; scoop out pulp, being careful to keep orange shells whole. Reserve shells. Press pulp through sieve to obtain juice. You will need about 1 cup juice to complete recipe.

In a saucepan, melt margarine. Add flour and cook for 1 minute, stirring constantly. Remove from heat and add orange zest and orange juice. Return to heat and bring to a very slow boil, stirring constantly. Simmer 2 minutes. Stir in artificial sweetener to taste and remove again from heat. Allow to cool. Whisk egg whites until stiff, and fold into cooled orange mixture.

If necessary, slice a thin layer off bottom of orange shells to allow them to stand. Pour orange mixture into shells, filling them about two-thirds full. Place shells in roasting pan and bake in hot oven until soufflé rises and is well browned. Just before serving, dust tops of oranges with artificial sweetener.

CHOCOLATE FANTASY

4 SERVINGS

1 envelope dietetic chocolate pudding mix
$\frac{1}{2}$ cup evaporated skim milk
1 $\frac{1}{4}$ cup black coffee
1 egg yolk, lightly beaten

Combine pudding mix, milk and coffee in a saucepan and cook, stirring over moderate heat until thickened. Remove from heat. Add egg yolk, stirring constantly. Return to heat for 1 minute. Pour into individual bowls and refrigerate.

PART FOUR

EXERCISE

CHAPTER ONE

I'm the product of an earlier age, an age when physical fitness was not considered essential to maintaining a good figure. Maybe that's why I used to be a little skeptical when people told me they enjoyed working out. To me, it seemed like a chore, particularly since I never considered riding, dancing or swimming exercise. For me that word always conjured up images of people in sweatshirts, stretching and groaning in agony. My attitude was always "Thanks but no thanks."

Then again it may be that my former negative feelings about exercise had to do with my physical problems. Perhaps without those problems I would have been one of the first to jump on the fitness bandwagon. I'm sure I would have given it a try. And maybe exercise would have kept me if not thin, at least in shape. The physical activity would have burned off extra calories and any such program would have occupied some of the time I spent feeling sorry for myself. Or eating. Or both.

Never mind. For years I hardly ever exercised, partly because I thought I'd hate it, partly because I was afraid of hurting myself. Now all that's changed. Today I know that some form of moderate exercise is essential to maintaining my weight. And if I can look forward to my exercise sessions you can too. But a word of caution:

Use your head before you go to work on your body.

First and most important, regardless of your age, and no matter how healthy and fit you *think* you are, don't begin an exercise program of any kind without getting an okay from your doctor. Remind him or her of any physical problems you have now or may have had in the past. Explain your goals and ask about low-risk activities that will help you meet them. Your physician might suggest that you undergo a series of tests before getting started. It is essential to follow his or her advice.

Because of my back problems, I had to be extra careful. I was afraid to devise an exercise program on my own (a bad idea for *anyone,* in my opinion), so I consulted Dr. Leroy R. Perry, a well-known and highly respected chiropractor who is president of the International Sports Medicine Institute in Los Angeles. He planned a routine for me that includes a brief series of simple exercises designed to improve general muscle tone, strengthen my back and upper body, and improve my posture. (If you want to subtract ten years and ten pounds in ten minutes, stand properly; I'll tell you how later on.) Dr. Perry also encouraged me to use the pool, not just for splashing but for aerobic swimming.

What a difference it's made. I wouldn't exactly call myself a fitness freak, but I've learned to enjoy the wonderful sense of well-being I experience after physical exertion. I love what I see happening to my body and I appreciate the fact that burning off additional calories through swimming makes it just that much easier to stay at 122 pounds.

One note of caution: Just because the following program was designed to be easy on *my* back, don't assume that the same activities will be equally appropriate for you. Even if you believe you have no physical weaknesses, discuss the exercises with your doctor before you attempt them.

STANDING UP FOR YOURSELF

The one thing all of us can improve without real physical exercise is our posture. Unfortunately, there's something about that word that makes people's eyes glaze over. I suppose it's because we were all nagged as children to stand up straight. The truth is, those well-intentioned naggers were onto something very important.

Slumping makes even a young woman look fatigued and defeated by life. Even if she has a great body, it will be concealed by bad posture, and if she's overweight, bad posture can make her look at least ten pounds fatter. The woman who carries herself as if she were beautiful *is* more beautiful.

Bad posture was never one of my problems. A lifetime in front of the camera is a sure cure for round shoulders. But Dr. Perry did give me some pointers on correct posture which are definitely worth passing on.

To start with, he suggests getting undressed and standing barefoot in front of a full-length mirror. Your weight should be evenly distributed on both feet. With your arms hanging loosely at your sides, try to stand so that an imaginary straight line would run from a midpoint between your ankles and knees upward, bisecting your pubic bone, your navel, your chest, your chin and your forehead. If you could draw *horizontal* lines connecting ankles, knees, hips, shoulders and eyes, they all would be level.

Now turn and look at yourself in profile. Ideally, you should be able to draw an imaginary *vertical* line from slightly in front of your anklebone, through the forward third of your knees, through your hipbone, slightly forward of your shoulder and up, bisecting your ear.

This alignment, says Dr. Perry, is close to perfect. If it doesn't come naturally, practice. Unless you have minor musculoskeletal problems (you'd already know about any major ones), proper alignment will soon begin to feel comfortable, and natural.

Finally, here's a technique you can use to remind yourself to stand tall and walk proud. It's done with mental imagery. Although Dr. Perry says that some of his patients—including many Hollywood stars and several Olympic athletes—balked when he first suggested the technique, they soon discovered that it works. Here it is:

First pick a bright color. Then close your eyes and imagine five helium-filled balloons in that color floating above your body. One is attached to the top of your head, one to each pectoral muscle, and one to the top of each hipbone. Get into the habit of associating your color with the imaginary balloons. Then, as you go about your day, each time you see your color visualize the balloons pulling tautly and gently, but firmly, lifting your head, your chest, your hips.

You'll discover that as your head lifts, neck tension eases. As your chest and pelvis rise, your shoulders and back relax. A wonderful sense of buoyancy will be immediately reflected in the way you sit, stand, move. In a few weeks you feel more graceful, confident, younger.

TONING, STRETCHING, FLEXING EXERCISES

I try to do the following exercises twice a day, once in the morning and again in the evening. They help tone muscles and improve flexibility, and I personally find them invigorating. Because many of them are designed to "decompress" the spine—to counteract the contraction that is the inevitable result of gravity—they also seem to make me taller. This may just be illusion, but at the very least I'm not getting any shorter!

1. MORNING STAR

This one helps stretch and limber your upper, middle and lower back. It also tones abdominal muscles while stretching the gluteals (your main rump muscles) and adding flexibility to hamstrings (the tendons behind your knees).

1. Lie on your back on a rug or carpet. (Never do this exercise on a soft surface or bed.) Your right arm should be stretched overhead and your left arm extended at a 90-degree angle to your body. Legs should be straight. Without tensing the muscles in your buttocks, tuck your tailbone under so that the pelvis tilts up. (Concentrate on using your abdominal muscles for this.)

2. Swing your left leg over and across your right leg.

3. Repeat, this time with left arm raised, right arm extended, and crossing right leg over left.

4. Do five sets; increase to ten sets after two weeks.

Important: During the first week, simply follow the instructions given above. During the following weeks, begin to stretch out your arms and legs and hold positions 2 and 3 for longer periods, finally working up to a full five seconds of stretching and extending arms and legs as far as possible.

2. ABDOMINAL CURLS

They look a little like sit-ups. They feel a little like sit-ups. They even flatten the tummy like sit-ups. But they're much easier on the spine, and by strengthening your lower abdominal muscles they also help support your back. P.S. You'll need a pillow for these.

Curl #1

1. Lie on your back on a rug or exercise mat with your legs fully extended, feet rotated so that toes point inward, heels slightly outward. Squeeze a pillow between your upper thighs, the higher the better. Fold your arms across your chest, and without tensing buttocks, tuck your tailbone under so that your pelvis tilts up.

2. In one continuous slow movement—still keeping the pillow in place between your upper thighs—raise your head enough to curl your chin into your neck; then tilt your nose toward your chest, and your forehead toward your abdomen. The lowest part of your shoulder blades should remain in contact with the floor even at the highest point of the curl.

3. Gradually uncurl back to starting position.

4. Repeat five times.

5. During the first week, simply complete the full movement. In the second week, pause briefly at the highest point of the curl. Gradually lengthen the duration of this pause until you are holding the position for a count of five.

Curl #2

With feet on floor, knees bent at a 30-degree angle, repeat Curl #1, steps 1 through 5.

Curl #3

With legs supported on a chair, repeat Curl #1, steps 1 through 5.

3. REVERSE SHOULDER SHRUGS

These easy-to-do exercises promote upper-body flexibility while realigning spine, neck and head. Since they also tend to reduce the negative effects of gravitational pull from the shoulders on up, Dr. Perry likens this series to the equivalent of a "natural postural facelift." You'll see, as your upper back becomes stronger and your shoulders stop rounding, you'll carry your neck and head more gracefully. As a result, your throat and face should begin to look firmer, better toned. A further benefit is that the exercise increases lung capacity, thereby improving circulation.

Shrug #1

1. Lean with your back resting lightly against a door. Your arms should be at your sides, your feet slightly rotated so that your toes point in.
2. Keeping your chest fully expanded, rotate your shoulders up, then back, then down as far as possible, as if to "grasp" the door between your shoulder blades. (Dr. Perry emphasizes that in order to get the slouch out of your upper back, shoulders should be rotated *backward* only, never forward.)
3. Hold for a count of five, then return to original position.
4. Repeat ten times.

Shrug #2

1. Lean against a door as in Shrug #1, but this time bend arms at elbows, touching hands to shoulders.
2. Keeping your chest fully expanded, rotate shoul-

ders up, then back, then down as far as possible, trying to "grasp" the door with your shoulder blades.

3. Hold for a count of five, then return to original position.

4. Repeat ten times.

Shrug #3

1. Lean against a door as in Shrug #1, but with your arms extended to the sides at shoulder level. Push out with your hands with as much force as possible.

2. Keeping your chest fully expanded and still pushing out with your hands, rotate shoulders up, then back, then down as far as possible.

3. Hold for a count of five, then return to original position.

4. Repeat ten times.

Note: For even greater benefit, increase to two sets of ten shrugs each after two weeks, and to three sets of ten after three weeks.

4. STANDING PELVIC TILT

This is another exercise done with a pillow. It flattens the tummy and helps realign a swayed lower back, thus making less of a protruding fanny. Dr. Perry says it's also a help in developing and maintaining better posture.

1. Place a pillow high up between your thighs. With your arms raised above your head, use your hands— palms against the wall—to support yourself at a 30- to 45-degree angle. Your feet should be flat on the floor. Keep your tailbone tucked under so that the pelvis tilts up.

2. Squeeze the pillow as hard as possible, using the muscles in your lower abdomen and upper thighs. Do *not* tense buttocks muscles.

3. Hold for a count of five.

4. Repeat ten times.

5. FACE SAVERS

This one helps promote better tone through your neck and jaws by reducing tension in your upper spine, neck and head. I always look more relaxed and rested after I do ten.

1. Standing straight and tall, clasp your hands behind your neck at the base.

2. Exerting smooth, steady pressure, try to push your head and neck back while resisting with your clasped hands.

3. Push/resist for a count of five.

4. Repeat ten times.

6. LEG SHAPER

This rock-in-place exercise is for you if you want toned thighs and calves, and generally better definition from ankles to hips. (Doesn't everyone?)

1. Stand straight and tall with your weight distributed on the heel of your left foot, the toes of your right.

2. Keeping your hips steady—no swinging or swaying—rock your weight to the heel of your right foot, the toes of your left. As you do, bring your right arm forward and your left arm back in typical walking fashion.

3. Now rock weight to the heel of your left foot, the toes of your right, bringing your left arm forward and your right arm back.

4. Repeat forty times.

AEROBIC EXERCISES—ARE THEY FOR YOU?

I never like to tell anyone what they should or shouldn't do. It's your life and you have to make your own decisions about how to live it. Nevertheless, I'll make an exception here and say that if you are in moderately good health, you should get in at least a few hours of aerobic exercise each week.

All exercises are *not* aerobic. The ones I've just described keep me stretched and flexible, but they are not aerobic. They don't keep my body in continuous motion for sustained periods; they don't build endurance; and they don't condition my heart and lungs, which is what aerobic exercise is all about.

For real fitness and endurance—the kind that helps build reserves of energy you never knew you had, you must consider aerobics. They can also be invaluable to any dieter, since they help speed the metabolism and burn calories faster.

If I sound like a convert, I suppose it's because I am. Everywhere I look I see the highly visible results of aerobic training. You must have noticed it too. Where did all the flab go? Women my age and older can have firm, sexy bodies. Eating properly is important but aerobic workouts are the real key.

Although jogging and aerobic dancing are popular in many parts of the country, neither is ideal for me because of all the foot-to-floor pounding, which places too much strain on my back.

But swimming! That's something else again. It's fun. There's no hard surface impact, just gentle gliding through water. You use your whole body, so it tones and streamlines all over. And because you're in constant motion, swimming provides the all-important benefit of cardiovascular conditioning. If you're going to go in for aerobic swimming in a big way, you may want to consider a health club, and of course, most Y's have pools.

Though it's safer than most other aerobic activities, even swimming can aggravate back problems. Dr. Perry, for example, insists that I wear a flotation device similar to a water-ski belt, with the strap turned to the back so there's more lift through the abdomen. Even if your spine has never given you a moment's discomfort do check with your doctor before taking the plunge. Go easy at the beginning; swimming too fast or too long the first few times out is just as risky as overdoing any other activity to which your body is unaccustomed. At first count lengths instead of laps. (A lap is up and back, a length is one way.) Psychologically it makes you feel you've done more.

How much and how often to swim, those are questions only you can answer, but exercise works only if it is done regularly. These days, since my body is fairly well conditioned, a half-hour three times a week seems fine. Some weeks I try for an extra day and some weeks when my schedule is very hectic I barely fit in two sessions. I *really* look forward to my pool time and am disappointed when I have to miss even a single session.

AQUA-AEROBICS

Sometimes, for a change of pace, or when I'd rather not get my hair wet, I substitute fifteen to thirty minutes of aqua-aerobics for laps. These exercises are always performed with my body in a vertical position, head above the water. I wear a flotation belt fastened loosely under my arms, or a swim vest, to minimize foot contact with the floor of the pool. Dr. Perry says that many aqua-aerobic exercises can be performed with almost anything that floats—a beach ball, a life preserver, even kick boards, one under each arm.

The three aqua-aerobics exercises that follow are only part of my routine; I'm including them just to give you an idea of what they are and how they work. Try them. If you enjoy them, ask the swim instructor at your health club or Y for a few more so that you'll have enough for a full-scale workout.

It's important to understand that these exercises are aerobic—meaning they promote endurance and cardiovascular fitness—*only* when done continuously, one exercise following another without a break. This takes practice, and it may be a while before you can perform them with the speed and continuity it takes to reap the cardiovascular benefits. In the meantime, as you work toward that goal, you'll be burning off loads of extra calories while toning and shaping those areas that probably need it most!

In aqua-aerobics, you should always stand (or rather float) straight and tall, with your chest held high and your tailbone tucked under. If you're not a good swimmer, make sure there's someone nearby who is. Don't go into deep water—it isn't necessary, you'll be fine in water that's shoulder-high. And remember, exercising with a friend is always more fun.

1. HIGH BENT-KNEE DRILLS

I begin and end every aqua-aerobic session with this exercise. It strengthens and tones arms, tummy, upper back and buttocks. A flotation device or swim vest is a must for this one.

1. Keeping your feet off the floor of the pool, "run" in the water, moving arms forward and backward, hands cupped toward each other. (Left knee up, right arm forward; right knee up, left arm forward.) The idea is to raise your knees as high as possible with each "step" you take. (I can get mine up as high as my waist now!)

2. Begin with three or four running steps. Gradually work up to a five-minute "run." It may take weeks or even months, but you'll make it.

2. HIGH KICKS

A thigh and arm firmer if there ever was one. Again you will need some form of flotation device.

1. Keeping your feet off the floor and rotating your arms in front-to-back circles for balance, kick your right leg out and up as high as possible.

2. Still rotating your arms, kick your left leg out and up as high as you can, as if you were in a chorus line.

3. Repeat, alternating legs.

4. Start with thirty seconds of high kicks. Work up gradually to two minutes.

Note: As you become stronger and your endurance increases, pick up speed until you are doing as many kicks per minute as possible.

3. BALLET DRILLS

This one is a terrific workout for hips, thighs, calves.

1. Stand straight and tall in the pool, left foot pointed like a ballet dancer's. Rotating your arms for balance, sweep right foot in a 180-degree arc in front of left ankle and back again; then sweep right foot in a 180-degree arc back and forth in front of left knee; finally, sweep right foot back and forth in front of left thigh.

2. Repeat, swinging right foot in 180-degree arcs *behind* left ankle, then knee, then thigh.

3. Now stand with right foot pointed and swing left foot in front of, and then behind, left ankle, knee and thigh, as above.

4. Start with one two-minute set; work up to three minutes, doing as many sets as possible.

OTHER AEROBIC OPTIONS

Obviously, swimming—both laps and aqua-aerobics—is *my* aerobic activity of choice, because it's least stressful to my back. But unless you too are afflicted with back problems, there's no reason why you shouldn't consider one or more of the many other aerobic options open to you.

Maybe you'd have more fun bicycling, either out of doors or on a stationary bike. The first gets you out on the open road in the fresh air. The second has the advantage of being weatherproof (no excuses for not exercising when it's raining or cold), and since you don't have to watch where you're going, you can read or watch TV while you pedal. A rowing machine offers many of the same advantages.

Then, of course, there's just plain walking. A leisurely stroll is better than nothing, but it's not very "aerobic." Better is to walk *briskly,* swinging or pumping your arms. To minimize the chance of injury, Dr. Perry suggests that you lean slightly forward as you stride, keeping your tailbone tucked under and pushing off with your rear foot. I'm told that carrying light wrist weights and/or strapping on ankle weights will enhance the training effect.

I haven't even begun to cover the wide range of aerobic exercises you might want to consider. There are probably dozens of them I haven't even heard of. The point is, any aerobic exercise will build energy, promote longevity, and best of all if you're dieting, burn calories!

If you are determined to get into the best shape possible, make an appointment with your doctor and discuss with him or her the pros and cons of the various aerobic activities and the best ways to get started. No matter what your physical problems or the present state of your health, there's at least one that's right for you.

But don't expect to fall in love immediately with the aerobic activity of your choice. Give it a chance to grow on you. It will, though it may take a while. And even after it has become an integral part of your life, expect. days when you just don't feel motivated to move. I know. Even now there are occasional days when I'd rather relax beside the pool than jump into it. But I'm getting better and better at resisting those impulses, and each time I do, I feel and look the better for it. Also, when you exercise when you really don't feel like it, you feel twice as virtuous afterward.

PART
FIVE

TO
SUM UP

CHAPTER ONE

The secret to living successfully as a thin person is very simple. *Think* of yourself as a slim, happy person, and let that definition be your guide. If you are satisfied with what you have become, then you can go on and maintain the new you with energy and enthusiasm. In my case, I no longer regard myself as the fat woman pictured in the *National Enquirer*. I don't deny that I was, I just concentrate on my new, active life which allows no time for unhealthy, self-indulgent behavior. And that includes eating too much. If you have now lost the weight you wished, you too can maintain your new slender figure by following a few simple rules.

The first requisite is to have faith in what you have accomplished. Erase those images of yourself as clumsy and overweight. Even if a few short months ago you were a Two-Ton Tony Galento, don't look back. Today you are a slender person and you must learn to adopt that new self-image.

In her book *Eating Disorders,* Dr. Hilde Bruch wrote about a phenomenon she termed "distortion of body image." Her research disclosed that women who had been heavy as teenagers tended to think of themselves as heavy even when they became slim adults. They have

never erased those old tapes and the danger is that some-
day they may allow themselves to live up to those negative images. They may regain the weight they lost because
they believe that their fat self is their real self. When I
hear women who look slim and fit complaining constantly about their weight, I'm never surprised to learn
that they were heavy as youngsters. I'm sure you know
people like that—maybe you're one yourself.

I wasn't overweight as a child, but the years I spent
struggling with fat in my forties left a pretty strong
impression on my psyche. There were times after I had
slimmed down when I had to remind myself that I was
not Madame de Large anymore. Even with the slender
evidence mirrored before me, a simple thing like a tight
skirt could throw me into a tizzy. Indeed, one did. It
was marked size six, and when I tried it on and the
zipper wouldn't close, I nearly had a fit. Though I had
been faithfully following my maintenance program I began
cursing myself for eating too much salad at lunch. Of
course the truth was my figure hadn't changed a whit.
The skirt was mismarked. It was a size four! But how
quickly I conjured up my old fat image—common but
dangerous behavior for someone who's just lost a great
deal of weight. The essential key to maintenance is to
concentrate on the present.

Follow my lead. Don't hold on to an outmoded out-
line of your shape. If your scale records a weight appropriate to your height, bone structure and age, chances
are you're looking great. So don't live in fear that you'll
revert to type. Today your "type" is trim and attractive,
but if you think of yourself as heavy or dumpy, others
may get that message, as may your own supersensitive
psyche. Believe me, you'll be a lot happier and have an
easier time staying thin if you focus your energies on
living your new vital and rewarding life.

One of the most heartening results of my own re-
naissance was a renewed interest in those around me,
particularly the ones I love most. No one is prouder of
what I've accomplished than my own family. When I
was lethargically dragging myself from one unrewarding

activity to another, I stopped thinking about anything other than how miserable I was. I lost sight of the most important people in my life, my children and my grandchildren. That's one of the worst side effects of losing self-esteem. When you're down on yourself, you tend to isolate yourself. The first real sign of my recovery came when I started thinking like a parent again. Now I revel in my children's accomplishments.

Michael, a gifted actor, has been working steadily in New York for years. He augments regular appearances on a popular TV soap opera with performances on and off Broadway. He and his wife, Brooke, an actress and producer, visit me often, but not often enough. My only regret is that I don't get to see Michael's daughters, my two oldest grandchildren, Laele and Naomi, as frequently as I'd like. My second son, Christopher, is working behind the camera as an editor in movies and television here in Los Angeles. His two boys, Caleb and Andrew, visit me all the time, allowing me to play Granny to my heart's content. My daughter Liza, who settled in upstate New York, has a brilliant career as a sculptress. In my entire art collection, there's nothing that means more to me than the bronze equestrian statuettes Liza presented to me a few years ago. In 1986, her bronze model of John Henry, the wonder horse, was selected for reproduction and sale in porcelain by the Newmarket Gallery. On Mother's Day 1986, Liza gave birth to my newest grandchild, Quinn. In my bedroom over the fireplace is a lovely oil portrait of my daughter and her baby boy, painted by her husband, Hap Tivey. The baby of the family, Maria Burton Carson, has settled in New York City, where she's raising her daughter, Eliza. When it's time, I'm sure Maria will return to work either as a model or in some new venture, but in the meantime she's free to experience the total joy of mothering, a privilege I often envy her.

Not only is it rewarding for me to watch my children's progress, it's equally satisfying for them to regard the new me. What a difference it makes to have a mother whom they can admire instead of pity, who can assist them instead of embarrass them. When Chris, who's inherited my love of sweets, wanted to lose weight, he asked for my diet and lost twenty-five pounds. Now he's devised his own version of my basic plan. The truth is, my kids don't need me, but I'm delighted I can be there for them if they do seek my advice. It's a wonderful feeling to be of help to your children, especially after they grow up and become independent.

In addition to finding new joy in my family, once I had defined the people and activities important to my new life, I discovered I had a great deal of energy to meet new friends and try new activities. As long as you too concentrate on your new self-image and self-respect, you will also find yourself making new acquaintances and assuming new roles, almost without trying. It's all part of the incredible expansion that comes with change.

In order to function best in your brave new world, it's essential to pick strong friends. You need supporters, not saboteurs. Sometimes it's not easy to distinguish one from the other. When you're fat, the world is divided into two groups—people who bug you and people who leave you alone. The funny thing is, supporters and saboteurs exist in either camp. The great thing is that the "new" you can differentiate between the two. When I was fat, friends did try to help me. Some thought they could do it best by keeping quiet and letting me do what I pleased until I came to my senses. Others nagged. Frankly, it didn't make much difference what anyone did, at least not until I myself decided to give up my self-defeating patterns of behavior.

Now that I've recovered, I find I do seek the company of people who tend to reinforce my new way of life. Here's a good example of what I mean. I had lunch with a visiting girlfriend a few weeks ago. In deciding what to eat, I was torn between a salad and the house specialty, a luscious chicken pie topped with a mile-high crust. "You should try the chicken pie," I told my companion. "It's fabulous." The waiter came over to take the order and my friend said, "I've heard your chicken pie is wonderful but I'll try it another day. Just let me have the fruit salad and cottage cheese." Without losing a beat, I closed my menu and said, "Give me the same." I'm not claiming that had my friend ordered the chicken pie I *definitely* would have followed suit, I'm simply noting that she made it easier for me not to. I know other women who would have had the chicken pie and followed it with dessert. I see those friends on occasions that don't involve eating. Also, I don't talk about food all the time. I used to. If I wasn't eating a meal, I was thinking about it. Today I practice sensible eating and "mental fasting."

Once my new habits were firmly established, I was able to lend others a hand. I became a supporter. It's a role I feel obliged and honored to take, for many reasons. Not long ago, I watched a television talk show on obesity. There were four people on the program. Three of them, two men and a woman, were recovered fatties. The fourth was a monstrously proportioned woman named

You need supporters, not saboteurs.

Mary Ann. Mary Ann claimed she had dieted almost all her life until she grew sick and tired of it. Her feeling was that she couldn't keep the weight off, so why should she go through life trying to be what she couldn't? Today, she asserted, she "enjoyed being fat." The other three questioned her position. The two men were firm but understanding. They felt that she should make an attempt to take off *some* weight. Their comments exhibited an honest concern stemming from their own experiences. The newly thin woman, on the other hand, was unbelievably cruel. She laid into Mary Ann with a vengeance, telling the woman she was just lying to herself and there was no way she could be anything but mis-

erable unless she lost weight. Her position was the an-
tithesis of support, one I could never take and, thank
heaven, one that was never taken with me. No matter
how happy she professed to be, Mary Ann was in pain.
You can't be content when you weigh so much you can't
sit in an ordinary chair. Although few fatties reach such
proportions, I think many people with past or present
weight problems have a secret fear they will. I'm sure
it's one reason why the audience laughed so nervously
throughout the telecast. I think we make obese people
the object of scorn because somewhere deep down we're
convinced it might happen to us. It can. And it did . . . to
me.

When I became obese, I used all the excuses—what
the hell, it's my body, it's my life. But God knows, I
was sensitive to what people said, and because I was a
movie star, I got away with more than the average obese
person. My presence continued to have
value . . . to others, if not to myself. That's not
usually the case. There is a lot of discrimination
toward fat people. Jobs are denied them and
judgments are made about them strictly on the
basis of size. Even my celebrity couldn't shield
me entirely. On the contrary, it fueled televised
jokes and continual magazine articles. Although
I never want to waste time dwelling on the negative aspects of the past, I do feel it's important
not to forget how easily fatties are hurt and to
remember to be supportive rather than destructive with
anyone dealing with a weight problem.

Become an expert on your new way of living.

Another rule for learning to enjoy living thin is to
get out of the house and keep busy. All the time I was
heavy, if I wasn't forced to go out by family demands
or work, I holed up at home. More specifically, in my
kitchen or in front of my TV. The minute I lost weight,
I wanted to go out, but even if you find it still a struggle,
you must make yourself circulate in public. Do whatever
it is you enjoy. And there are so many activities to
choose from. I love to dance. I suppose it's part of my
upbringing, when going out in the evening meant dinner

and dancing. Now I can concentrate more on the latter, and that includes discos. If you have young children, get involved with their school—go to PTA meetings or help organize after-school activities. Become involved with politics. You don't have to marry a senator—you can make changes in our government far more effectively just sitting on local committees. The point is to focus your new life on new interests and activities, not the refrigerator or the television.

When you leave the security and comfort of your "nest," you are, of course, taking a risk. But maintaining a healthy self-esteem requires taking risks. And if you are circulating for the first time after losing weight, the risk has its own reward. Your friends—and even your enemies—will be stunned by the new you. I know the kick I got the first few times I appeared before the media when I reached 122 pounds. Sure, there was some vanity involved. All women like to look attractive. But far more important was the reaffirmation of the direction my life had taken. There is no greater boost to the self-esteem than to have others acknowledge that you are in control.

A good way to stay in control is to become an expert on your new way of living. It's not as difficult as you might think. When you are watching your diet, you are assessing what you eat. Because of this, any serious dieter becomes somewhat of an authority on food. Don't fight it. Learn all you can. When I started out, I did just that. I read books and talked to dietitians and doctors. I got so I couldn't look at a piece of food without having its caloric/carbohydrate/nutritional content flash before my eyes. A simple piece of cake was broken down into flour, sugar, water, eggs, each with its specific nutritional value. Now that my eating pattern has been firmly established I'm less conscious about the nutritional content of each bite, but this knowledge still helps keep me from bingeing or even sitting around too long dreaming about candy bars whose nutritional value is zilch. More important, if you know the caloric content of what you're munching, you'll be less likely to become an involuntary nibbler.

Just as you should enjoy your new knowledge about food, you should also develop expertise about other aspects of your physical being. Become a pro at your wardrobe and makeup. Find out what beauty and health products suit you. Learn which styles are flattering to you and which are not. Again, I'm not talking about extremes. You don't have to sit around with your nose in fashion magazines or support your local dress store singlehandedly in order to exhibit a lively interest in your appearance. I'm talking about a sensible program of acquiring information that will keep you looking your best. *Care* about yourself enough to know what's good for you.

One thing that's good for everybody is physical activity. I've already discussed its importance during the diet. It is equally important to maintenance. Again, become an expert on which exercises are healthiest and which of those are best for you. A decade ago there was a great flurry of interest in physical well-being. *Aerobics* became a buzzword and old-fashioned calisthenics took a back seat. Over the next few years, we learned that aerobic exercise was healthier when it was "low-impact" and combined with the tried-and-true calisthenics. Ironically, while the adult population is now gung-ho into physical fitness, recent studies have shown that their kids have grown fatter and flabbier. In fact, schoolchildren today have forty percent more body fat than fifteen years ago! They're sitting around in front of the television and eating junk food rather than going outside for active play. To add to the problem, schools themselves have cut back on their physical education programs in favor of additional time for academics. Consequently, it's imperative for parents to make some sort of activity part of the home scene. Don't just encourage children to participate in team sports, get out there and jog or walk or bike with them.

The hardest thing about performing any physical activity is to make sure you stick to a weekly program. Just because you've reached your ideal weight, don't get lazy. Make sure you do whatever you have to in order to exercise regularly. Some people motivate themselves by joining health clubs or exercise classes. If you don't wish to spend the money, try taking a brisk walk every day. But don't leave it to chance. Pick a time and make it inviolable. Once you establish a set pattern of behavior, you can adhere to it more easily than if you approach it with a slapdash mentality. If you can find someone to join you in this, all the better. I know of three women who got together about five years ago and established their own "health club." There are no dues and there are no instructors. These ladies meet every morning, rain or shine, at 6:30 A.M. and walk briskly for one hour. Then they return home and assume their appointed tasks. Rather than being "tired out" from their early activity, they're actually energized and feel the benefits all day.

Finally, in order to maintain the new you, you must avoid excess fats and sugars. Regard these as the enemy, which, in fact, they are. Examine the diet of those schoolchildren I just mentioned, and you'll find they eat a preponderance of foods saturated with fats and filled with sugar. This is where your newly found nutritional expertise can pay off for you and your family. When you're aware that certain foods offer nothing but empty calories, it's a little easier to substitute foods that do.

Maintenance based on good eating habits, regular exercise and a firm focus on your new and active life can make the present so enjoyable that you will have no trouble adopting these habits for the rest of your slim and fruitful life.

CHAPTER TWO

When she was nearly seventy years old, Sophie Tucker, "the last of the Red Hot Mamas," said, "From birth to age eighteen, a girl needs good parents. From eighteen to thirty-five, she needs good looks. From thirty-five to fifty-five, she needs a good personality. From fifty-five on, she needs good cash."

Bravo, Sophie! With one glaring omission, the old girl hit it right on the button. I would add that from birth onward every person has to have a strong sense of self-worth. That's the one currency you can cash in during every stage of life.

I ought to know.

I'm in the final stage of Ms. Tucker's life equation and have come through all the others if not with flying colors, at least with a good sense of my own worth.

I was lucky. I had good parents. Some people aren't as fortunate. For whatever reasons they grow up feeling unloved. That's tough on self-esteem, but early neglect—whether real or perceived—is not insurmountable. It can even build character. Given the fact I was a celebrity before I reached my teens, the best parenting in the world could not prevent some distortion in my self-image. Constantly faced with adult situations and denied the companionship of my peers, the fact is that

I stopped being a child the minute I started working in pictures. I didn't understand how deeply it affected me until years later, when I went to the Betty Ford Center. There, I thought through my early experiences in order to live the rest of my life in the healthiest way possible.

This is probably a good idea for all people, whether or not they feel they have significant problems. After all, it is easier to restrain negative impulses if we understand why they occur. That way we can each take control if not of the circumstances of our lives, at least over the way we handle them.

When I derailed in Washington, I had no idea that my real problem was a lack of self-worth and that all the food in the world would not fill up my inner feelings of emptiness. You have to be mighty low to think that a hot fudge sundae is going to make everything all right. But for many middle-aged women, it's a classic response to unhappiness. Fortunately, now that you've read about my experiences, you know that there are many healthier and more satisfying solutions.

One is to try to reward yourself for achieving and maintaining your ideal weight. At least once a month save up to buy yourself something you want for the new you. I'm not suggesting you have to pop into Cartier or Tiffany for expensive baubles. Far from it. You don't have to spend a great deal of money to get satisfaction. You can opt for costume jewelry, lacy underwear or just a picture frame for a photograph of you looking thin and chic. (Don't forget to change the photograph to keep up with your image!) The point is, whatever you buy yourself doesn't have to be costly; you merely have to want it.

Another tip to encourage maintenance and healthy self-esteem is to try a new physical activity each month. Experiment with skis or skates. Enroll in a dance or swimming class. If you know how to swim, learn a new stroke. One of my friends took a scuba diving course at the Y. To learn the techniques, she and her classmates donned all the equipment and jumped into the indoor pool. Now she's graduated to the ocean and has become such an enthusiast she wants to work for a marine biology firm. The main thing, though, is to expand your horizons while enjoying some new form of exercise. Ballroom dancing is a popular activity. Not long ago, the tango had a revival. People took lessons and started gliding across the dance floors to the syncopated Argentinean beat. Really, activities like this don't seem like exercise, just fun.

You may not wish to keep up a particular activity, but it doesn't hurt to give it a try. You'd be surprised how enthusiastic you can become about something learned late in life. I read about an eighty-year-old woman who participated in the Boston Marathon. She said she became interested in running when she was in her seventies!

Another tip to make maintenance eating more fun is to try a new diet recipe each week. Different approaches to the same foods help keep your taste buds alive and kicking. Some newspapers offer daily recipes that either are calorie-conscious in themselves or can easily be adapted to my diet. I clip out the ones that are particularly appealing and give them a try. Or you can challenge yourself by creating your own low-calorie dishes. It's also a great idea to sit down once a week and write down menus for the upcoming seven days. That way you will be less tempted to stray from your regimen.

Any new and different ideas (as long as they are constructive) promote enthusiastic maintenance. Remember I told you that I dyed my hair blond a few years ago? I did it as a lark, and while I didn't stay blonde, I had a helluva good time being one for a while. If there's something you've always wanted to do but didn't, I urge you to try it now. I know a physician who was so busy he never had time to indulge his creative side. He was well into his sixties when he took up the piano, something he'd always yearned to do. He's not a Vladimir Horowitz by any means, but he takes as much pleasure struggling through Beethoven's *"Für Elise"* in his living room as any concert pianist playing Scarlatti sonatas in Carnegie Hall. Many people have enriched their lives by taking up an instrument. And for people whose interests are musical but not necessarily instrumental, there's nothing nicer than joining a choir. Again, it doesn't have to be the Tanglewood Festival Chorus, it can be a small local group. Or, if you have a literary bent, try writing the story you've been threatening to put onto paper all these years. If you need guidance, most cities offer courses in creative writing. Take one. Or try a course in photography, or art. I've dabbled in painting, and while my efforts remain spotty, I have friends who have become excellent artists. Some have gone "commercial" and their works fetch good prices! Though it is a good feeling, you don't have to make money at what you elect to do. The point is, the more you do, the more alive you will feel.

But even if you try everything that I advise, there will be times when you will find yourself dying for hot fudge or whatever your particular weakness is. That's when you must do two things: First, force yourself to wait thirty minutes. That should do the trick, but if it doesn't then *reach out*. Call a friend. Even if you don't want to, make yourself seek the help you need. You're not a failure because you crave something or even if you give in and binge. As long as you get help and go right back to your diet or maintenance program, you should still consider yourself a success.

Finally, give of yourself. I am active in the cause against AIDS. Even before my friend Rock Hudson died, I acknowledged this terrifying scourge. I was angered by the loud silence involving AIDS. The discrimination, the stigma. I thought, I'm doing the same thing, so get out there and do something. So I did! I was actively involved, but Rock's death brought the cause into my heart. I don't think anyone should sit by idly while there is work to be done to make this world better and safer.

My cause is the fight against AIDS, but there are many organizations that need help. There is too much famine, disease, war and political oppression for anyone to sit back and worry solely about his or her waistline. My God, nothing will raise your self-esteem as much as

helping others. It will make you like yourself more and make you more likeable. We can't all be Mother Teresas but each of us can try to make our little corner of the earth a little better.

Today I think I am happier than I have ever been. There have been other times in my life marked with joy, like the blissful years I shared with Mike and Richard. But this is the first time that I've made my own happiness. It didn't fall into my lap because I was young or lovely or famous. Nor did it come about because I was in love with a man. This happiness wasn't "bestowed" on me, I earned it.

═══

The point is, the more you do, the more alive you will feel.

═══

In overcoming seemingly insurmountable obstacles, I learned that my oversized body wasn't the biggest barrier to my self-esteem. To regain a healthy sense of self-worth I first had to break down old fears and doubts and anxieties. Only then was I able to reshape my image successfully. Now, my exterior and interior are in harmony. I really feel as good as I look. And dammit, I know I look good.

I've worked hard to reach this state and that's why it's the sweetest victory of all. But the war isn't over. There are so many things I want to do, I can scarcely believe it. Professionally, I've worked on three films in three years and am at the point where I can barely keep up with proposals for new projects. I'm also involved in a major business venture. Though I do take great satisfaction in these endeavors, I think I'm proudest of

my charitable contributions. I've raised millions of dollars for the American Foundation for AIDS Research. And I'm not stopping here. I won't stop until that hideous disease is conquered.

I guess what I'm trying to say is, after decades of being a movie star, a name in the headlines, I've become an active and productive person. I think I've proven that anyone can change her life around and make it work. You only have to try.